Acknowledgments

Acknowledgment is gratefully made to the following publishers, authors, and agents for permission to reprint these works. Every effort has been made to determine copyright owners. In the case of any omissions, the Publisher will be pleased to make suitable acknowledgments in future editions.

"The Cat Ate My Gymsuit" by Paula Danziger. Copyright © 1974 by Paula Danziger. Published by Delacorte Press.

"Coping with an Aggressive Dog" by Michael W. Fox. *Boys' Life* magazine, August 1987, p. 6. Reprinted by permission of Michael W. Fox

"The Phantom Tollbooth" from *The Phantom Tollbooth* by Norton Juster. Copyright © 1961 by Norton Juster. Published by Random House, Inc.

"The Trade" reprinted from *Ghost in the Bleachers* by David E. Griffith, © 1997. Used with permission of Lowell House, a division of NTC/Contemporary Publishing Group, Inc.

"Just the Beginning" from *Just the Beginning* by Betty Miles. Copyright © 1976 by Betty Miles. Published by Alfred A. Knopf, Inc. Reprinted by permission of the author.

"Bats Incredible!" by Arlene Schnippert. Copyright © 1987 by the Worldwide Church of God. Reprinted from *Youth* magazine, November/December 1987. All rights reserved.

"Twenty-One Balloons" from *The Twenty-One Balloons* by William Pene du Bois. Copyright © 1947 by William Pene du Bois, renewed © 1975 by William Pene du Bois. Used by permission of Viking Penguin, a division of Penguin Putnam, Inc.

"You Kids Are All Alike" from *Signposts to Achievement* by Ira E. Aaron, et al. Copyright 1975 by Scott, Foresman and Company. Reprinted by permission of Addison-Wesley Educational Publishers, Inc.

"Snow Bound" from *Snow Bound* by Harry Mazer. Copyright © 1973 by Harry Mazer. Used by permission of Delacorte Press, a division of Random House, Inc.

"How to Be Somebody" by Shirley M. Dever. *Listen* magazine, July 1985. Reprinted by permission of the author.

"Sounder" from *Sounder* by William H. Armstrong. Text copyright © 1969 by William H. Armstrong. Used by permission of HarperCollins Publishers.

"She Wanted to Read" from *She Wanted to Read* by Ella Kaiser Carruth. Copyright © 1966 by Abingdon Press. Used by permission.

"Song of the Stranger" reprinted from *Song of the Stranger* by Angela Tung. © 1999. Used with permission of Lowell House, a division of NTC/Contemporary Publishing Group, Inc.

"Skin: The Bag You Live In" from *Blood and Guts: A Working Guide to Your Own Insides* by Linda Allison. Copyright © 1976 by The Yolla Bolly Press. By permission of Little, Brown and Company (Inc.).

"Seward's Warning" from *The Eyes of the Amaryllis* by Natalie Babbitt. Copyright © 1977 by Natalie Babbitt. Reprinted by permission of Farrar, Straus & Giroux, Inc.

"A Long Way to Whiskey Creek" from *A Long Way to Whiskey Creek* by Patricia Beatty. Copyright © 1971 by Patricia Beatty. Published by William Morrow and Company, Inc.

"Rescued Whales" by Andrew McPhee. Special permission granted, *Current Science* ®, copyright 1987. Published by Weekly Reader Corporation. All rights reserved.

"The Black Cauldron" from *The Black Cauldron* by Lloyd Alexander. Copyright © 1965 by Lloyd Alexander. Reprinted by permission of Henry Holt and Company, LLC.

"A Summer to Die," excerpt from *A Summer to Die* by Lois Lowry. Copyright © 1977 by Lois Lowry. Reprinted by permission of Houghton Mifflin Company. All rights reserved.

"The Martial Arts," an adapted excerpt from *The Martial Arts* by Susan Ribner and Dr. Richard Chin. Copyright © 1978 by Susan Ribner and Dr. Richard Chin. Reprinted by permission of the authors.

"Island of the Blue Dolphins" from *Island of the Blue Dolphins* by Scott O'Dell. Copyright © 1960, renewed 1988 by Scott O'Dell. Reprinted by permission of Houghton Mifflin Company. All rights reserved.

"The Native American Meets the Horse" adapted from *Out of the Saddle: Native American Horsemanship* ™, by GaWaNi Pony Boy, ISBN 1-889450-37-4. Copyright 1998 BowTie Press, a division of Fancy Publications Inc., 3 Burroughs, Irvine, CA 92618.

Contents

	To the Student	1
Sample		
	Snowflake Bentley	4
1	Ready for High Speeds	8
2	The Cat Ate My Gymsuit	
	by Paula Danziger	12
3	The Man in the Water	16
4	Women at War	20
5	Coping with an Aggressive Dog	
	by Michael W. Fox	24
6	The Phantom Tollbooth	
	by Norton Juster	28
7	Black Holes	
	by Henry and Melissa Billings	32
8	The Trade	
	by David E. Griffith	36
9	Go for the Gold	
	by Henry and Melissa Billings	40
10	Just the Beginning	
	by Betty Miles	44
11	Bats Incredible!	
	by Arlene Schnippert	48
12	The Twenty-One Balloons	
	by William Péne du Bois	52
13	Exploring the Last Frontier	56
14	To Build a Fire	
	by Jack London	60
15	You Kids Are All Alike	64
16	Snow Bound	
	by Harry Mazer	68
17	How to Be Somebody	
	by Shirley Dever	72

18 Sounder
    by William H. Armstrong   76

19 She Wanted to Read
    by Ella Kaiser Carruth   80

20 The Birth of the Blues
    by Henry and Melissa Billings   84

21 Song of the Stranger
    by Angela Tung   88

22 Skin: The Bag You Live In
    by Linda Allison   92

23 Seward's Warning
    by Natalie Babbitt   96

24 A Long Way to Whiskey Creek
    by Patricia Beatty   100

25 Rescued Whales
    by Andrew McPhee   104

26 The Black Cauldron
    by Lloyd Alexander   108

27 A Summer to Die
    by Lois Lowry   112

28 The Martial Arts
    by Susan Ribner and Dr. Richard Chin   116

29 Island of the Blue Dolphins
    by Scott O'Dell   120

30 The Native American Meets the Horse
    by GaWaNi Pony Boy   124

Words-per-Minute Table   130

Graphs

    Reading Speed   131

    Comprehension   132

    Critical Thinking   133

    Vocabulary   134

How Am I Doing?

    Lessons 1–10   135

    Lessons 11–20   136

    Lessons 21–30   137

To the Student

You probably talk at an average rate of 150 words a minute. But if you are a reader of average ability, you read at the rate of 250 words a minute. So your reading speed is already nearly twice as fast as your speaking or listening speed. This example shows that reading is one of the fastest ways to put verbal information into your mind.

The following chart illustrates what an increase in reading speed can do for you.

It shows the number of books read over a period of 10 years by various types of readers. Compare the number of books read by a slow reader and the number read by a fast reader.

Reading Drills is for students who want to read faster and with greater understanding. By completing the 30 lessons—reading the selections and doing the exercises—you will certainly increase

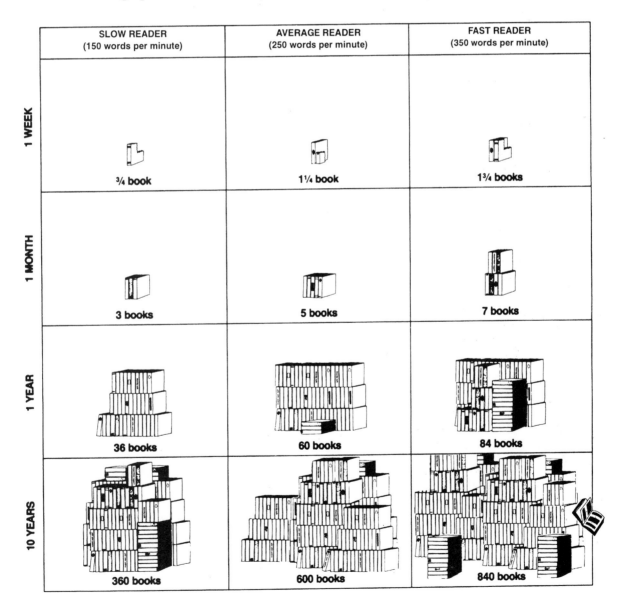

	SLOW READER (150 words per minute)	AVERAGE READER (250 words per minute)	FAST READER (350 words per minute)
1 WEEK	¾ book	1¼ book	1¾ books
1 MONTH	3 books	5 books	7 books
1 YEAR	36 books	60 books	84 books
10 YEARS	360 books	600 books	840 books

your reading speed, improve your reading comprehension, and sharpen your critical thinking skills.

How to Use This Book

About the Book

Reading Drills, Middle Level contains 30 lessons. Each lesson begins with a fiction or nonfiction reading selection. After reading the selection, record your reading time and reading speed. The lesson also includes exercises in reading comprehension, critical thinking, and vocabulary, as well as personal response questions. The reading comprehension and vocabulary exercises help you understand the selection. The critical-thinking exercises help you reflect on what you have read and how the material relates to your own experience. At the end of the lesson, the personal response questions give you the opportunity to respond to various aspects of the story or article.

The Sample Lesson

The first lesson in the book is a sample lesson that your class or group will work through together. It helps you understand how the lessons are organized. The sample lesson explains how to complete the exercises and score your answers. Sample answers and scores are printed in lighter type. If you have any questions about completing the exercises or scoring them, this is the time to get the answers.

Working Through Each Lesson

1. Begin each lesson by reading the introduction. It prepares you to read the selection. As you read the selection itself, you are timed. Either you or your teacher will set a timer when you begin reading the selection. When you finish reading, record your time on the Reading Time line in the box at the end of the selection. Then find your reading speed on the Words-per-Minute table on page 130 and record it on the Reading Speed line in the box. Finally, record your speed on the Reading Speed graph at the end of the book. Keeping track of your reading speed will help you monitor your progress.

2. Next complete the exercises. The directions for each exercise tell you how to mark your answers. When you have completed all four exercises, use the answer key provided by your teacher to check your work. Record your scores after each exercise. Then fill in your scores on the appropriate progress graphs at the back of the book. Your teacher will help you interpret your progress on the graphs.

3. Check your progress. To get the most benefit from working through these lessons, you need to take charge of your own progress in improving your comprehension, critical-thinking, and vocabulary skills. The graphs and charts help you keep track of your progress, but you need to study them from time to time to see whether your progress is satisfactory or whether you need additional work on some skills. The How Am I Doing? questions on pages 135–137 provide guidelines to help you assess your progress and determine what types of exercises you are having difficulty with.

Lessons

Sample   Snowflake Bentley

> The snowflake is unique in all the world. No two snowflakes are alike, and each one is beautiful in its own way. No one was ever more fascinated with snowflakes than Wilson "Snowflake" Bentley, who was, himself, unique in all the world.

The winter wind swept through the tiny village of Jericho, Vermont. Then the first snow of the 1880–1881 season began to fall. Most people took that as a good enough reason to stay inside. But Wilson "Willie" Bentley had other ideas. He pulled on his boots. Then he grabbed his coat, cap, and mittens and headed for the door.

Willie loved everything about the outdoors, but he especially loved the snow. Of course, other 15-year-olds loved snow too. But Willie's love went beyond sledding and snowball fights. He wanted to actually study the white stuff. So into the driving storm Willie trudged, carrying the new microscope his mother had given him. He caught a few snowflakes and placed them gently under his microscope. Looking down at them magnified thousands of times, Willie gasped. The snowflakes were all so beautiful, and they were all different. Their unique qualities, however, were lost forever when the snowflakes melted. Somehow, Willie thought, he had to capture their beauty.

At first Willie thought he could sketch each snowflake. So he set up a workshop in an unheated woodshed. He borrowed a piece of black velvet from his mother and used the swatch of fabric to catch snowflakes. After gathering a few prize samples, he would dash back to the woodshed and place the snowflakes under his microscope. Then Willie would sketch as fast as he could. But he was never quite fast enough. The snowflake always melted before he could draw an accurate picture.

Willie's odd behavior caught everyone's attention. His father felt that Willie was wasting his time. Charlie, Willie's older brother, thought he was nuts. Most of the neighbors in Jericho shared that opinion. Still, Willie would not give up. He hoped that someday people would understand the beauty he saw in snowflakes. But for the moment his most urgent concern was finding a better way to preserve that beauty.

He spent hours striving to improve his sketches. Then one day he had a bright idea. He saw an advertisement for a special camera that could be attached to a microscope. With a camera like that, Willie could photograph snowflakes. Unfortunately, the camera cost $100. In the 1880s, that was a lot of money to a poor farmer like Willie's father. Besides, a man would have to be crazy to spend $100 so that his son could take pictures of snow.

Mr. Bentley wasn't crazy, and he still couldn't make sense of his son's hobby, but he loved to see Willie happy. So he and his wife cut some corners to save money. On Willie's 17th birthday, Mr. and Mrs. Bentley presented their son with the special camera.

No one had ever photographed snowflakes before, so there were no books or manuals explaining how to go about it. Willie had to resort to trial and error. On January 15, 1885, he finally got it right. He took a perfect photograph of a snowflake.

Willie, who had come to be nicknamed Snowflake, wanted to do nothing but photograph snowflakes. And for the next 46 years that is exactly what he did.

He never married. He never moved from the farmhouse where he was born. Snowflake Bentley managed to survive by doing some farming and writing magazine articles.

Willie lived for the next snowstorm. Townspeople got used to seeing him outdoors in the foulest weather. If it began snowing during mealtime, he would stop eating and dash outside. If a storm lasted all night, Willie would forget about sleeping. He couldn't bear the thought that some great snowflake might escape his lens.

By 1931 Willie had photographed 5,381 snowflakes. People all over the world knew of his work. His book, *Snow Crystals*, was published in November 1931. Still, for Willie, now 66 years old, a new winter meant new snowflakes. In early December, he gave a lecture in a neighboring town. That night a terrible blizzard struck. Friends strongly urged Willie to stay in town. But Willie would have none of it. He loved wild snowstorms; they often yielded the best photos. So he wrapped a scarf around his neck and walked the six miles back to his house. When he finally staggered into his farmhouse, he was shaking all over.

The next day Willie fell ill. At first he insisted that he would get better. But he didn't. He only got worse. Finally, Willie's nephew called in the doctor. But it was too late. Snowflake Bentley died two days before Christmas. ■

✔ **Enter your reading time below. Then look up your reading speed on the Words-per-Minute table on page 130.**

Reading Time _____

Reading Speed _____
Enter your reading speed on the Reading Speed graph on page 131.

Comprehension

Put an **X** in the box next to the correct answer for each question or statement. Do not look back at the selection.

1. Willie Bentley's story begins in the winter of 1880–1881 when Willie was
   - ☒ a. 15 years old.
   - ☐ b. 10 years old.
   - ☐ c. 7 years old.

2. Where did Willie set up his workshop?
   - ☐ a. in the kitchen of his house
   - ☒ b. in an unheated woodshed
   - ☐ c. in a friend's house

3. Willie caught his snowflakes
   - ☐ a. in his hand.
   - ☒ b. on a piece of black velvet.
   - ☐ c. on a cold piece of glass.

4. Willie couldn't draw an accurate picture of a snowflake because
   - ☒ a. it would melt too quickly.
   - ☐ b. his microscope was not good.
   - ☐ c. his hand was so cold that it was difficult for him to draw.

5. Willie received his special camera on his
   - ☒ a. 17th birthday.
   - ☐ b. 15th birthday.
   - ☐ c. 20th birthday.

6. Before getting his camera, Willie tried to preserve the beauty of snowflakes by
   - ☐ a. writing articles about them.
   - ☐ b. storing them on ice.
   - ☒ c. sketching them.

7. Willie never slept
   - ☐ a. when it was dark outside.
   - ☐ b. more than four hours a night.
   - ☒ c. during a snowstorm.

8. Wilson Bentley was the first person ever to
   - ☒ a. photograph snowflakes.
   - ☐ b. walk six miles in a snowstorm.
   - ☐ c. study snowflakes under a microscope.

✎ ___8___ Number of correct answers
Enter this number on the
Comprehension graph on page 132.

Critical Thinking

Put an **X** in the box next to the best answer for each question or statement. You may look back at the selection if you'd like.

1. The purpose of the first paragraph is to
   - ☐ a. describe winter in Vermont.
   - ☐ b. express an opinion about Willie's odd behavior.
   - ☒ c. reveal that Willie liked to be out in the snow.

2. Which of the following statements best expresses the main idea of the selection?
   - ☒ a. Wilson Bentley devoted his life to capturing snowflakes on film.
   - ☐ b. Wilson Bentley put together a book about snowflakes.
   - ☐ c. Wilson Bentley loved snow.

3. From what you read you can conclude that
   - ☐ a. Snowflake Bentley was a lonely man.
   - ☐ b. Snowflake Bentley died in poverty.
   - ☒ c. almost everyone in Jericho, Vermont, knew Snowflake Bentley.

4. What was the effect of Willie's six-mile walk home through a blizzard in December 1931?
   - ☒ a. He became ill and died.
   - ☐ b. Friends urged him to stay in town.
   - ☐ c. He published a book of his photographs called *Snow Crystals.*

5. Which word best describes the kind of father Mr. Bentley was.
   - ☐ a. strict
   - ☐ b. crazy
   - ☒ c. loving

6. Which of the following is a statement of opinion rather than fact?
   - ☐ a. By 1931 Willie had photographed 5,381 snowflakes.
   - ☒ b. Besides, a man would have to be crazy to spend $100 so that his son could take pictures of snow.
   - ☐ c. On Willie's 17th birthday Mr. and Mrs. Bentley presented their son with the special camera.

7. Which statement below best describes Willie's life?
   - ☐ a. He was sad and lonely because he never married.
   - ☒ b. He lived alone but was happy doing the thing he loved best.
   - ☐ c. He became a famous photographer and had a book published.

8. From Willie Bentley's actions you can predict that if you asked him about his final walk home in the blizzard, he would say that he
   - ☐ a. was frightened all the way home.
   - ☒ b. enjoyed seeing all the snowflakes along the way.
   - ☐ c. regretted walking home in the blizzard.

✎ ___8___ Number of correct answers
Enter this number on the Critical
Thinking graph on page 133.

Vocabulary

Each numbered sentence contains an underlined word or phrase from the selection. Following are three definitions. Put an **X** in the box next to the best meaning of the word or phrase as it is used in the sentence.

1. So into the driving storm Willie <u>trudged</u>, carrying the new microscope.
   - ☒ a. walked with effort
   - ☐ b. stumbled
   - ☐ c. hurried

2. Looking down at them <u>magnified</u> thousands of times, Willie gasped.
   - ☐ a. repeated
   - ☐ b. made smaller
   - ☒ c. made larger

3. Their <u>unique</u> qualities, however, were lost forever when the snowflakes melted.
   - ☐ a. similar
   - ☒ b. one-of-a-kind
   - ☐ c. unusual

4. The snowflake always melted before he could draw an <u>accurate</u> picture.
   - ☐ a. inexact
   - ☒ b. correct
   - ☐ c. pretty

5. He spent hours <u>striving</u> to improve his sketches.
   - ☐ a. drawing
   - ☐ b. forgetting
   - ☒ c. trying

6. Willie had to <u>resort to</u> trial and error.
   - ☒ a. use
   - ☐ b. learn about
   - ☐ c. give up on

7. Townspeople got used to seeing him outdoors in the <u>foulest</u> weather.
   - ☒ a. nastiest
   - ☐ b. oddest
   - ☐ c. nicest

8. He loved wild snowstorms; they often <u>yielded</u> the best photos.
   - ☐ a. withheld
   - ☐ b. observed
   - ☒ c. provided

✎ _____8_____ **Number of correct answers Enter this number on the Vocabulary graph on page 134.**

Personal Response

Why do you think Willie Bentley photographed snowflakes?

[Write down reasons why Willie Bentley may have taken pictures of snowflakes.]

_____

_____

Just before he died, Willie Bentley walked home through a terrible blizzard. Describe a time when you were out in a powerful storm.

[Tell about an experience you had in a storm similar to the one Bentley was in.]

_____

_____

1 | Ready for High Speeds

What does it take to be a race car driver? Are driving skills enough, or is there more to it than that?

The track at the Indianapolis 500 Speedway is 2½ miles long. At speeds of about 250 miles per hour, you can whip around the track in about 38 seconds. You make a left turn, then drive a short straight stretch. After another left turn, there's another straight run; then you must turn left again. The track is packed with other cars. At any moment, a car could cut in front of you and crash into the wall. Or you could crash. You make another left turn and go into the straight!

Then you do it all again—199 more times—as fast as you can push your car. Auto racing may be the most exciting sport in the world.

What kind of a person do you have to be to drive a race car? One thing you need is nerve—and plenty of it. At 250 miles per hour, a crash is never more than a split second away. You're driving a car that's being pushed to the limit. The engine is turning 10,000 times per minute, hour after hour. Most cars used for street driving would blow up if pushed past 7,000 turns per minute. The wheels, the clutch, or any part of the car could let go at any moment. But you stay composed and dive into the next turn.

The human heart beats about 75 times per minute. During a race, a driver's heartbeat quickly increases to 160, even 180! In races like the Grand Prix, a driver's heart hammers at 180 beats per minute—nonstop for two hours!

Most people would feel completely exhausted. But you can't rest during a race. Race car drivers have to train their bodies. Formula 1 drivers' average heart rate while resting is down to about 63 beats per minute. Their bodies also make better use of the oxygen they breathe. This means that even at their high heart rate during a race, drivers still have energy left at the end of the race. And they may need it if their cars' steering starts to wear out.

Drivers also have to be in good shape. Body fat takes blood away from the brain and muscles. It also keeps the body warm. In a hot race car, an overweight person would feel too warm. Race car drivers also need to have flexible bodies. It is less likely that they will be hurt in a crash if their bodies can bend.

Good eyes are another "must." Drivers have to see things that are far away and be able to quickly judge how far away they are. They also have to see close-up things, like the oil gauge. Drivers also must be able to see things clearly out of the corners of their eyes. Drivers need this kind of vision to see, for example, a wheel come off the car to the right.

Seeing objects ahead of time isn't enough. A driver has to decide what to do about what he or she sees—and do it—in an instant. How fast a person can act is called *reaction time*. Anyone who drives a car needs good reaction time, but in a race, a driver has to think much faster. Even $\frac{1}{100}$ of a second can make a huge difference. At 200 miles per hour, that split second equals a whole car length!

A driver can test his or her reaction time on a machine. On the machine, eight buttons are set into a desktop shaped in a half circle. The driver has to hit the buttons that light up, one after the other. The buttons are wired to a computer, which measures the driver's reaction time. Indianapolis 500 drivers are very quick. Formula 1 drivers, who must race on turning, twisting roads, are even quicker.

One more thing race car drivers need is a good attitude. They have to go into races with the idea that they're going to win. Some drivers do this by thinking back to times they have felt the best, the most ready, and the most confident. They set their minds to feel the same way again. They take time before a race to get their minds ready for racing.

When you think about it, these sound like good tips for succeeding at just about anything. Stay calm. Concentrate. Think fast. Keep an eye on everything that's happening around you. Keep your body in good shape. And whatever you do, keep a good attitude. With all this going for you, how can you lose? ■

✔ Enter your reading time below. Then look up your reading speed on the Words-per-Minute table on page 130.

Reading Time _____

Reading Speed _____

Enter your reading speed on the Reading Speed graph on page 131.

Comprehension

Put an ✘ in the box next to the correct answer for each question or statement. Do not look back at the selection.

1. How long is the track at the Indianapolis Speedway?
   ☐ a. 500 miles
   ☐ b. 25 miles
   ☐ c. 2½ miles

2. To drive a race car you must have
   ☐ a. a lot of patience.
   ☐ b. an indifferent attitude.
   ☐ c. plenty of nerve.

3. Most cars used for ordinary street driving would blow up if their engines were pushed past
   ☐ a. 5,000 turns per minute.
   ☐ b. 7,000 turns per minute.
   ☐ c. 10,000 turns per minute.

4. During a race, a driver's heartbeat may jump as high as
   ☐ a. 180 beats per minute.
   ☐ b. 75 beats per minute.
   ☐ c. 63 beats per minute.

5. Race car drivers must limit the amount of body fat they have because fat
   ☐ a. takes blood away from the brain and muscles.
   ☐ b. decreases the body's natural heat.
   ☐ c. could hinder the driver's ability to move freely in the car.

6. How fast a driver can act is called
   ☐ a. preventive action.
   ☐ b. decision time.
   ☐ c. reaction time.

7. At the rate of 200 miles per hour, each split second it takes for a driver to act is equal to
   ☐ a. one car length.
   ☐ b. two car lengths.
   ☐ c. three car lengths.

8. Testing has shown that the race car drivers who can act the quickest are
   ☐ a. Indianapolis 500 drivers.
   ☐ b. Formula 1 drivers.
   ☐ c. stock-car drivers.

✎ _____ Number of correct answers
Enter this number on the Comprehension graph on page 132.

Critical Thinking

Put an **X** in the box next to the best answer for each question or statement. You may look back at the selection if you'd like.

1. The purpose of the first paragraph is to
   - ☐ a. describe the track at the Indianapolis 500 Speedway.
   - ☐ b. convey a mood of fear.
   - ☐ c. inform you how dangerous it is to race on the Indianapolis 500 Speedway.

2. Which statement best expresses the main idea of the selection?
   - ☐ a. Besides good driving skills, a race car driver must be fearless, be in top physical shape, and have good reaction time and a good attitude.
   - ☐ b. Race car drivers must have exceptional driving skills to drive at such high speeds on tracks packed with other cars.
   - ☐ c. Driving a race car is very dangerous; a crash is never more than a split second away.

3. In the Indianapolis 500 race, how many times must drivers drive around the track?
   - ☐ a. 500
   - ☐ b. 200
   - ☐ c. 199

4. If a race car driver does not have a good reaction time, you can predict that he or she will
   - ☐ a. drive slower.
   - ☐ b. drive faster.
   - ☐ c. have an accident.

5. Race car drivers still have plenty of energy left after a long, hard race because
   - ☐ a. their bodies make good use of the oxygen they breathe.
   - ☐ b. they get extra sleep before a race.
   - ☐ c. they have learned to relax during a race.

6. Which of the following is a statement of opinion rather than fact?
   - ☐ a. The track at the Indianapolis 500 Speedway is 2½ miles long.
   - ☐ b. Auto racing may be the most exciting sport in the world.
   - ☐ c. The human heart beats about 75 times per minute.

7. Drivers need to be able to bend their bodies easily so they
   - ☐ a. can squeeze into their small race cars.
   - ☐ b. can do proper warm-up exercises.
   - ☐ c. will be less likely to be hurt in a crash.

8. Compared to other people, the average heart rate of a Formula 1 race car driver is
   - ☐ a. lower.
   - ☐ b. about the same.
   - ☐ c. higher.

✎ _____ Number of correct answers
Enter this number on the Critical Thinking graph on page 133.

Vocabulary

Each numbered sentence contains an underlined word from the selection. Following are three definitions. Put an **X** in the box next to the best meaning of the word as it is used in the sentence.

1. But you stay <u>composed</u> and dive into the next turn.
   - ☐ a. excited
   - ☐ b. calm
   - ☐ c. nervous

2. During a race, a driver's heartbeat quickly <u>increases</u> to 160, even 180!
   - ☐ a. jumps up
   - ☐ b. rises slowly
   - ☐ c. drops down

3. Most people would feel completely <u>exhausted</u>.
   - ☐ a. refreshed
   - ☐ b. worn out
   - ☐ c. dedicated

4. This means that even at their high heart rate during a race, drivers still have <u>energy</u> left at the end of the race.
   - ☐ a. confidence
   - ☐ b. active strength
   - ☐ c. fuel

5. Race car drivers also need to have <u>flexible</u> bodies.
   - ☐ a. very strong
   - ☐ b. somewhat small
   - ☐ c. easy-to-bend

6. One more thing race car drivers need is a good <u>attitude</u>.
   - ☐ a. driving record
   - ☐ b. way of thinking
   - ☐ c. knowledge of the track

7. Some drivers do this by thinking back to times they have felt the best, the most ready, and the most <u>confident</u>.
   - ☐ a. prepared
   - ☐ b. uncertain
   - ☐ c. sure

8. When you think of it, these sound like good tips for <u>succeeding</u> at just about anything.
   - ☐ a. doing well
   - ☐ b. doing poorly
   - ☐ c. making an attempt

✎ _____ **Number of correct answers**
Enter this number on the Vocabulary graph on page 134.

Personal Response

Why do you think auto racing has become so popular?

_____

_____

Auto racing can be dangerous. Do you think it should be banned? Explain why or why not.

_____

_____

_____

2 | The Cat Ate My Gymsuit

by Paula Danziger

The Cat Ate My Gymsuit tells the story of an overweight girl and the problems she has in school and with her family. In this passage from the book, you get a glimpse at some of the difficulties she faces in her life.

School went on as usual. I kept getting good grades in everything but gym. My anonymous letters to the Student Council suggestion box were ignored. Lunches continued to be lousy. We were only up to the Civil War in history class.

It was different in some ways, though. I didn't sit alone at lunch anymore. I sat with some of the kids from Smedley. Ms. Finney's classes were still great, but the rest of the classes seemed even more boring than they were before she came. We kept asking the teachers to be more like her, but they made faces and told us to keep quiet. We talked out in classes more and asked more questions, but they didn't like that. We even asked some of them to join Smedley, but they said things like "What are you doing? Getting your heads shrunk?" and "My contract doesn't say I have to stay after school past last period."

What changed a lot was my home. It got even worse. My father has a horrible temper. He doesn't hit, but he yells. Even worse, he says awful things to me, like "I don't care if you get good grades. You do stupid things. Why do I have to have a daughter who is stupid and so fat? I'll never get you married off."

My mother would try to tell him to stop, but he wouldn't listen. They'd get into a fight and she'd start to cry and then go get a tranquilizer.

Then my little brother, Stuart, would cry and run for his teddy bear. While all this was happening, my father would scream at me. "Look at what you've done. We'd never fight if it weren't for you. Apologize." By that time, I'm crying. It usually ended with me running upstairs, slamming my door, throwing myself on my bed, and rocking back and forth. My mother would come in and hug me and tell me everything would be O.K., but that I really should lose some weight and look like everyone else.

I hated it. That's what usually went on in my house but, as I said, things got much worse.

In a way, it was because of Smedley. We did lots of neat stuff in there, and I wanted to try some of it at home.

One day in Smedley we broke up into groups and told each other how we saw each other and felt about each other. I was really excited. Nobody said that they hated me. They said I was smart and nice, but too quiet and shy. No one made fun of me. They didn't say I was skinny and beautiful, but they didn't tell me I was ugly and fat either. So I thought that maybe it would be good to try it at home.

My mother was all for it. I had told her about what we were doing in Smedley, and she really dug it, because she said it was making me different. I didn't tell her how scared I still was, though. I wanted her to be proud of me.

So one night at dinner, she explained that she wanted us all to sit around and talk like a family.

My father said, "I've worked hard all day for this family, Lily. Isn't that enough? I don't have to talk to all of you too, do I?"

Mom very quietly said, "Martin, I think it's important. Please."

So he said, "O.K. . . . a little while."

Mom and I cleared off the dishes, and then we went into the living room, where my father was watching television. Stuart was sitting on the floor, stuffing pits into the hole in Wolf, his teddy bear. Stuart watches a lot of commercials, and he once saw that oranges are supposed to keep you healthy. He used to try to put whole oranges in Wolf, but things got pretty sticky, so we convinced him that pits are best for bears.

My father frowned and said, "Let the kid stay here. He's part of the family too. And anyway, I want to talk to him about his stupid thumbsucking and that idiot teddy bear."

Stuart held Wolf in his arms and started to suck his thumb. "I love Wolf. He's my friend. He never yells at me."

"Look, kid. You're four years old. What are you going to be? Forty, hugging that bear and sucking your thumb? You'll never get a job that way." ∎

✔ Enter your reading time below. Then look up your reading speed on the Words-per-Minute table on page 130.

Reading Time _____

Reading Speed _____

Enter your reading speed on the Reading Speed graph on page 131.

Comprehension

Put an **X** in the box next to the correct answer for each question or statement. Do not look back at the selection.

1. In school the narrator got good grades in
   ☐ a. everything but history.
   ☐ b. only gym.
   ☐ c. everything but gym.

2. Ms. Finney's classes were
   ☐ a. great.
   ☐ b. boring.
   ☐ c. terrible.

3. The narrator's father often
   ☐ a. loses his temper.
   ☐ b. hits her.
   ☐ c. praises her.

4. When her parents fought, the narrator's mother would cry and then
   ☐ a. run to her room and slam the door.
   ☐ b. get a tranquilizer.
   ☐ c. yell at her husband.

5. Who or what is Wolf?
   ☐ a. the family's pet dog
   ☐ b. Stuart's teddy bear
   ☐ c. Stuart's nickname

6. According to a commercial Stuart saw, what are supposed to keep you healthy?
   ☐ a. vitamins
   ☐ b. bananas
   ☐ c. oranges

7. One evening, the narrator's mother wanted the family to
   ☐ a. discuss the narrator's weight problem.
   ☐ b. go to the movies together.
   ☐ c. sit and talk like a family.

8. Stuart loved his teddy bear mostly because it
   - ☐ a. was soft and cuddly.
   - ☒ b. never yelled at him.
   - ☐ c. talked to him.

✎ _____ Number of correct answers
Enter this number on the Comprehension graph on page 132.

Critical Thinking

Put an ✗ in the box next to the best answer for each question or statement. You may look back at the selection if you'd like.

1. The word that best describes the mood or feeling of this story is
   - ☐ a. cheerful.
   - ☐ b. sad.
   - ☐ c. funny.

2. Who is the narrator of this story?
   - ☐ a. an outside observer
   - ☐ b. Stuart's sister
   - ☐ c. Stuart

3. What is Smedley?
   - ☐ a. a rival high school
   - ☐ b. a nearby town
   - ☐ c. an after-school group

4. Which word best describes the narrator's home life?
   - ☐ a. busy
   - ☐ b. unhappy
   - ☐ c. contented

5. The narrator's father is mean to her because he thinks she
   - ☐ a. does not respect him.
   - ☐ b. is a troublemaker.
   - ☐ c. is stupid and fat.

6. Which of the following is a statement of opinion rather than fact?
   - ☐ a. Lunches continue to be lousy.
   - ☐ b. My anonymous letters to the Student Council suggestion box were ignored.
   - ☐ c. We were only up to the Civil War in history class.

7. The people at Smedley made the narrator feel
   - ☐ a. worse.
   - ☐ b. frustrated.
   - ☐ c. better.

8. Compared to her father, the narrator's mother treated her
   - ☐ a. better.
   - ☐ b. about the same.
   - ☐ c. worse.

✎ _____ Number of correct answers
Enter this number on the Critical Thinking graph on page 133.

Vocabulary

Each numbered sentence contains an underlined word from the selection. Following are three definitions. Put an ✗ in the box next to the best meaning of the word as it is used in the sentence.

1. My anonymous letters to the Student Council suggestion box were ignored.
   - ☐ a. silly
   - ☐ b. unlikely
   - ☐ c. unsigned

2. Lunches continued to be lousy.
   - ☐ a. sudden
   - ☐ b. terrible
   - ☐ c. short

3. "My <u>contract</u> doesn't say I have to stay after school past last period."
   - ☐ a. illness
   - ☐ b. owner
   - ☐ c. agreement

4. "Look at what you've done. We'd never fight if it weren't for you. <u>Apologize</u>."
   - ☐ a. accept a gift
   - ☐ b. admit your mistake
   - ☐ c. refuse to speak

5. Mom and I <u>cleared off</u> the dishes, and then we went into the living room.
   - ☐ a. threw
   - ☐ b. took
   - ☐ c. placed

6. Stuart watches a lot of commercials, and he once saw that oranges are <u>supposed</u> to keep you healthy.
   - ☐ a. believed
   - ☐ b. unable
   - ☐ c. prepared

7. He used to try to put whole oranges in Wolf, but things got pretty sticky, so we <u>convinced</u> him that pits are best for bears.
   - ☐ a. dissolved into
   - ☐ b. made to believe
   - ☐ c. acted out a story

8. "And anyway, I want to talk to him about his stupid thumbsucking and that <u>idiot</u> teddy bear."
   - ☐ a. sweet
   - ☐ b. silly
   - ☐ c. old

✎ _____ **Number of correct answers**
Enter this number on the Vocabulary graph on page 134.

Personal Response

What do you think will become of the narrator after she finishes high school? Use your imagination and write four to six sentences to describe what her life might be like.

_____

_____

_____

_____

I know how the narrator feels because

_____

_____

_____

3 | The Man in the Water

Most heroes are ordinary people who do something extraordinary. From that moment on, they are no longer ordinary. Arland Williams was such a person.

On January 13, 1982, a severe snowstorm hit Washington, D.C. The temperature fell to the mid-teens. Driving snow made it hard to see. Flights out of Washington's National Airport were delayed while snowplows cleared the runways. Air Florida Flight 90, with its 79 passengers, was no exception. It was originally scheduled to depart at 2:15 P.M. Clearing the runways, however, took over an hour. At 3:37, the pilot was finally allowed to move the plane into position for takeoff, but 15 other planes were lined up ahead of it. Another 20 minutes went by before Flight 90 could roll out onto the runway.

While Flight 90 was waiting for the runways to be plowed, the ice that had formed on its wings was removed. But new ice began to form immediately. As the pilot waited for the 15 other planes to take off, the ice grew heavier. Ice buildup on a plane's wings is dangerous. It makes the plane heavier and disturbs the normal flow of air over the wings. Despite the fresh layer of ice, Flight 90 roared down the runway when its turn came at 3:59 P.M.

As the jet took off, it shuddered. Something was wrong. It was not gaining altitude as it should. One of the passengers, who was also a pilot, said, "We're not going to make it."

Meanwhile, traffic on the Fourteenth Street Bridge over the Potomac River was heavy. It was rush hour, and the workers who lived outside the city were headed home. Suddenly the blue, green, and white form of an Air Florida 727 appeared out of the clouds. Flight 90 was going down, and it was heading straight for the crowded bridge. The motorists on the bridge could do nothing but watch in horror as the airplane fell from the sky and smashed across the northbound lane. The tops of several cars were sheared off. Four motorists were killed before the plane plunged into the frigid Potomac.

Rescue workers arrived on the scene quickly. Their searchlights revealed a hideous sight. Many of the passengers could be seen still strapped in their seats at the bottom of the Potomac. Only six passengers were still alive. They clung to a piece of the tail section that stuck out of the water. One of the people was a balding man with a large mustache. He seemed to be more alert and less severely injured than any of the others.

Speed was essential if the six people were to be saved. A person can survive only a few minutes in such cold water. The rescue was made difficult by the fact that there was only enough room for one helicopter to get between the Fourteenth Street Bridge and another bridge nearby.

A rescue helicopter arrived and quickly lowered its lifeline and flotation ring to the balding man. The man grabbed it, but instead of using it himself, he passed it on to one of the other passengers. As that person was lifted out of the freezing water, the balding man fought to keep his grip on the tail section. His body temperature was dropping, and the numbing cold of the water was sapping his strength. When the rescue helicopter returned, the lifeline was again dropped to him. Bystanders watched in amazement as the man once again passed the lifeline on to someone else. For the second time, he was giving up a chance to save himself in order to allow another person to be saved.

After a nerve-racking 10 minutes, the three other passengers had been taken safely to the shore. Only the balding man was left in the river. But when the helicopter returned, he was gone. He had been in the icy water too long.

For several days, the selfless hero was known simply as "the man in the water." No one knew who he was. But when the passenger list was compared with the description of the man, it was determined that he was Arland Williams, a 46-year-old bank examiner from Atlanta, Georgia.

When Arland Williams boarded Flight 90, he was an ordinary person on an ordinary flight. There was nothing special about him. But at 4:01 P.M. on a stormy January day, when the plane he was on slammed into a bridge and tumbled into the Potomac, Williams chose to risk his life to save the lives of others. The "man in the water" became a national hero. He had given up his life so that others might live. ■

✔ Enter your reading time below. Then look up your reading speed on the Words-per-Minute table on page 130.

Reading Time _____

Reading Speed _____

Enter your reading speed on the Reading Speed graph on page 131.

Comprehension

Put an **X** in the box next to the correct answer for each question or statement. Do not look back at the selection.

1. The plane crash took place in
   - ☐ a. Atlanta.
   - ☐ b. Florida.
   - ☐ c. Washington, D.C.

2. What delayed Air Florida Flight 90 from taking off earlier?
   - ☐ a. The runways had to be cleared of snow.
   - ☐ b. The plane had to be refueled.
   - ☐ c. The plane needed some engine repair.

3. Flight 90 crashed into the Potomac River
   - ☐ a. as it was attempting to land.
   - ☐ b. right after takeoff.
   - ☐ c. 30 minutes after takeoff.

4. Immediately after the crash, there were only
   - ☐ a. two passengers alive.
   - ☐ b. six passengers alive.
   - ☐ c. five passengers alive.

5. Besides people on Flight 90, others killed as a result of the crash were
   - ☐ a. rescue workers.
   - ☐ b. spectators on the shore.
   - ☐ c. motorists on the bridge.

6. The rescue was made more difficult because there
   - ☐ a. weren't enough rescue workers.
   - ☐ b. were no rescue boats available.
   - ☐ c. was only enough room for one rescue helicopter.

7. Who was Arland Williams?
   - ☐ a. a bank examiner
   - ☐ b. a rescue worker
   - ☐ c. the copilot of Flight 90

8. Arland Williams died because he
   - ☐ a. had suffered head injuries in the crash.
   - ☐ b. had been in the icy water too long.
   - ☐ c. did not know how to swim.

✎ _____ Number of correct answers
Enter this number on the Comprehension graph on page 132.

Critical Thinking

Put an **X** in the box next to the best answer for each question or statement. You may look back at the selection if you'd like.

1. The author probably wrote this article in order to
   - ☐ a. describe the passengers' terrifying experience on Flight 90.
   - ☐ b. relate the story of an ordinary man who became a hero.
   - ☐ c. identify "the man in the water."

2. The purpose of the first paragraph is to
   - ☐ a. convey a fearful mood.
   - ☐ b. explain the impact of the weather on Flight 90.
   - ☐ c. inform you about the effect of severe weather on air travel.

3. Which of the following best states the main idea of the selection?
   - ☐ a. Arland Williams, an ordinary person, became a hero when he died in the Potomac River after twice passing his lifeline on to save others.
   - ☐ b. Arland Williams died in the icy Potomac River after the plane he was on crashed on takeoff.
   - ☐ c. A bank examiner from Georgia became a hero when he died putting the lives of others ahead of his own.

4. Based on what you've read, you can conclude that the
   - ☐ a. accident could not be prevented.
   - ☐ b. plane carried too many passengers.
   - ☐ c. long wait on the runway played a part in the crash of Flight 90.

5. The crash of Flight 90 was caused by
   - ☐ a. driving snow that made it hard to see.
   - ☐ b. ice buildup on the plane's wings.
   - ☐ c. the failure of one of the jet engines.

6. Which of the following is a statement of opinion rather than fact?
   - ☐ a. Arland Williams was an ordinary person.
   - ☐ b. Arland Williams was a 46-year-old bank examiner from Atlanta, Georgia.
   - ☐ c. For several days, the selfless hero was known simply as "the man in the water."

7. You can predict that if Arland Williams had been lifted out of the water first,
   - ☐ a. most of the others clinging to the tail section would have died.
   - ☐ b. he would have jumped back in to save other passengers.
   - ☐ c. he would have died anyway.

8. Which event happened first?
   - ☐ a. Snowplows cleared the runways.
   - ☐ b. Ice that had formed on the wings of the plane was removed.
   - ☐ c. The pilot moved Flight 90 into position for takeoff.

✎ _____ Number of correct answers
Enter this number on the Critical Thinking graph on page 133.

Vocabulary

Each numbered sentence contains an underlined word from the selection. Following are three definitions. Put an **X** in the box next to the best meaning of the word as it is used in the sentence.

1. Despite the fresh layer of ice, Flight 90 roared down the runway when its turn came at 3:59 P.M.
   - ☐ a. on the other hand
   - ☐ b. in spite of
   - ☐ c. because of

2. As the jet took off, it shuddered.
   - ☐ a. shook severely
   - ☐ b. climbed higher
   - ☐ c. slowed down

3. It was not gaining altitude as it should.
   - ☐ a. speed
   - ☐ b. time
   - ☐ c. height

4. Their searchlights revealed a hideous sight.
   - ☐ a. dreadful
   - ☐ b. strange
   - ☐ c. appealing

5. He seemed to be more alert and less severely injured than any of the others.
   - ☐ a. comfortable
   - ☐ b. confused
   - ☐ c. lively

6. Speed was essential if the six people were to be saved.
   - ☐ a. impossible
   - ☐ b. necessary
   - ☐ c. unimportant

7. A person can survive only a few minutes in such cold water.
   - ☐ a. continue to live
   - ☐ b. help themselves
   - ☐ c. manage to swim

8. His body temperature was dropping, and the numbing cold of the water was sapping his strength.
   - ☐ a. freezing
   - ☐ b. draining
   - ☐ c. restoring

✎ _____ **Number of correct answers**
Enter this number on the Vocabulary graph on page 134.

Personal Response

Why do you think Arland Williams passed the lifeline to other passengers? Explain what may have motivated his heroic act.

_____

_____

Do you think anyone is capable of being a hero if a situation requires it? Explain your answer.

_____

_____

_____

4 | Women at War

There were countless heroes in the Vietnam War. Many of them were women. Although they did not fight in combat, these women faced danger every day as they carried out their vital jobs. This selection tells part of their story.

The Vietnam War was the longest war in United States history. It was the least popular war too. It was the only war the United States ever lost.

Between 1961 and 1973, more than 3.3 million Americans served in Vietnam. More than 58,000 of them died. The names of the dead are engraved on the Vietnam Veterans Memorial. This V-shaped, black granite wall is in Washington, D.C. People who see this memorial may be surprised by one fact. The wall names 13 women. But in all, 65 American women died in the Vietnam War.

More than 7,000 military women served in Vietnam. At that time, women did not fight in combat. They did not fly fighter planes. Most were nurses in MASH units. These units were often in war zones, so they were often attacked. The nurses faced danger again and again.

Army nurses had to deal with more than danger. They had to deal with their patients' pain and suffering. These nurses treated more than 153,000 wounded soldiers. Some soldiers were crippled for life, and many others died. As they died, the last face they saw was often the face of a nurse.

The nurses' job was heartbreaking. They treated so many men. Their patients came and went so quickly that, at times, patients' faces became a blur. Nurses tried to remember each one, but they could not. Sometimes, though, one face would stand out. It might be due to the man's cries of agony. It might be because of his last whispered words. Or it might be his look of

fear. Years after the war, nurses still had trouble shaking these painful memories.

Connie Curtley was a nurse in Vietnam. Her memories of the war are painful. Her strongest memory is the smell of dirty uniforms. Curtley often had to cut these uniforms off wounded men. "I can smell that smell just like it was happening right now . . . ," she said. At times, Curtley treated so many wounded men that her own clothes became soaked in blood.

Thousands of civilian women also volunteered to help in the war. Many of them served with the Red Cross. They brought food, medicine, and other supplies to those in need. Other women worked for private relief groups. Women also worked for the United States government and for the press.

These women, too, faced danger in Vietnam. Some of them died. One government worker died when the American Embassy in Saigon was bombed. A mine killed one female journalist. Gunfire killed another. Three missionaries were killed in a hospital raid. Four women died as prisoners of war.

One of the worst tragedies took place on April 4, 1975. The U.S. forces had left Vietnam. A group of women had planned a mission called Operation Babylift. They feared that orphaned children left in Vietnam would die there. So they tried to take these children out of the country to safety. Sadly, their plane crashed. Thirty-eight women and 100 children were killed.

The Vietnam Veterans Memorial honors 13 of the women who died in the war. But Diane Carlson Evans, a former Army nurse in

Vietnam dreamed of a memorial to honor all of the women who served there. Evans began planning it as early as 1983. It would take 10 years for her dream to materialize.

Evans formed the Vietnam Women's Memorial Project in 1984. Workers on the project had much work to do. They had to get Congress to approve the idea. They also had to design the memorial. American sculptor Glenna Goodacre planned a stunning sculpture of four bronze figures. The sculpture features three Vietnam-era women. One of the women tends a wounded soldier.

Workers on the project also had to find a site for the statue. They chose a spot next to the Vietnam Veterans' Memorial. The statue would remind visitors of women's role in the war.

Evans's group still had to get funding for the memorial. Over the years, project workers raised $2.5 million. Finally, the statue was built. It was unveiled on Veterans Day, November 11, 1993. Thousands of people came to the opening ceremony. They came to thank all of the brave women who served in Vietnam.

For the first time in American history, a memorial to honor women's service to their country was dedicated in the nation's capital. The statue not only celebrates the women's courage and loyalty; it also reminds all people of the huge human toll that war always takes. ∎

✔ **Enter your reading time below. Then look up your reading speed on the Words-per-Minute table on page 130.**

Reading Time _____

Reading Speed _____

Enter your reading speed on the Reading Speed graph on page 131.

Comprehension

Put an **X** in the box next to the correct answer for each question or statement. Do not look back at the selection.

1. The Vietnam War was the
   - ☐ a. only war the United States ever lost.
   - ☐ b. shortest war in U.S. history.
   - ☐ c. most popular war in U.S. history.

2. The Vietnam War took place between
   - ☐ a. 1961 and 1973.
   - ☐ b. 1941 and 1945.
   - ☐ c. 1949 and 1953.

3. How many women died in the Vietnam War?
   - ☐ a. 13
   - ☐ b. 65
   - ☐ c. 110

4. Most of the women in the Vietnam War were
   - ☐ a. Red Cross volunteers.
   - ☐ b. nurses in MASH units.
   - ☐ c. journalists.

5. Besides constant danger, the worst hardship Army nurses had to deal with was
   - ☐ a. the hot, sticky weather.
   - ☐ b. poor living conditions.
   - ☐ c. their patients' pain and suffering.

6. Where is the Vietnam Women's Memorial located?
   - ☐ a. Vietnam
   - ☐ b. New York City
   - ☐ c. Washington, D.C.

7. The Vietnam Women's Memorial was finally unveiled in
   - ☐ a. 1993.
   - ☐ b. 1984.
   - ☐ c. 1975.

8. The Vietnam Women's Memorial is intended to honor all the
   - ☐ a. women who died in the Vietnam War.
   - ☒ b. women who served in the Vietnam War.
   - ☐ c. nurses who served in Vietnam.

✎ |____| Number of correct answers
Enter this number on the Comprehension graph on page 132.

Critical Thinking

Put an **X** in the box next to the best answer for each question or statement. You may look back at the selection if you'd like.

1. The author's main purpose in writing this selection was to
   - ☒ a. inform you of the important role women played in the Vietnam War.
   - ☐ b. explain why the Vietnam War was the only war the United States ever lost.
   - ☐ c. persuade you that women should not fight in combat.

2. Which of the following is the most important idea concerning the role of the nurses in the war?
   - ☐ a. They did not have to fight in combat.
   - ☐ b. Most nurses served in MASH units.
   - ☐ c. Nurses had to deal with danger and their patients' pain and suffering.

3. Why didn't women fight in combat during the Vietnam War?
   - ☐ a. They were not trained to fight.
   - ☐ b. They were not permitted to fight.
   - ☐ c. They were afraid to fight.

4. Which event happened last?
   - ☐ a. The Vietnam Women's Memorial was built.
   - ☐ b. The United States' military forces left Vietnam.
   - ☐ c. The Vietnam Veterans Memorial was built.

5. A spot next to the Vietnam Veterans Memorial was chosen as a site for the Vietnam Women's Memorial because
   - ☐ a. it was the only good site available.
   - ☐ b. it would remind visitors to the Veteran's Memorial of women's role in the war.
   - ☐ c. Congress decided to put it there.

6. Based on what you read in the third paragraph you can conclude that
   - ☐ a. women still may not fight in combat.
   - ☐ b. women may now fight in combat.
   - ☐ c. only nurses may fight in combat.

7. Which of these groups of women does *not* fit with the other two?
   - ☐ a. Red Cross volunteers
   - ☐ b. Army nurses
   - ☐ c. government workers

8. Which sentence correctly restates the following: "The statue not only celebrates the women's courage and loyalty; it also reminds all people of the huge human toll that war always takes."
   - ☐ a. Women are honored by the statue for their service in the war.
   - ☐ b. The statue is dedicated to all those who served and died in the war.
   - ☐ c. The statue represents women's bravery and helps us remember that war costs many lives.

✎ _____ Number of correct answers
Enter this number on the Critical Thinking graph on page 133.

Vocabulary

Each numbered sentence contains an underlined word from the selection. Following are three definitions. Put an ✘ in the box next to the best meaning of the word as it is used in the sentence.

1. The names of the dead are <u>engraved</u> on the Vietnam Veterans' Memorial.
   - ☐ a. carved on a surface
   - ☐ b. painted
   - ☐ c. printed

2. At that time, women did not fight in <u>combat</u>.
   - ☐ a. armed fighting
   - ☐ b. a major war
   - ☐ c. the regular Army

3. It might be due to the man's cries of <u>agony</u>.
   - ☐ a. relief
   - ☐ b. surprise
   - ☐ c. unbearable pain

4. Thousands of <u>civilian</u> women also volunteered to help in the war.
   - ☐ a. those who enlisted in the armed forces
   - ☐ b. those unfit for the armed forces
   - ☐ c. those not in the armed forces

5. It would take 10 years for her dreams to <u>materialize</u>.
   - ☐ a. be denied
   - ☐ b. become an actual fact
   - ☐ c. become nightmares

6. They had to get Congress to <u>approve</u> the idea.
   - ☐ a. think about
   - ☐ b. give permission for
   - ☐ c. develop

7. They also had to <u>design</u> the memorial.
   - ☐ a. raise money for
   - ☐ b. build
   - ☐ c. plan out

8. American sculptor Glenna Goodacre planned a <u>stunning</u> sculpture of four bronze figures.
   - ☐ a. strikingly beautiful
   - ☐ b. extremely large
   - ☐ c. shocking

✎ _____ **Number of correct answers**
Enter this number on the Vocabulary graph on page 134.

Personal Response

Why do you think it was not until 1993 that a public memorial was dedicated to honor women's service to their country?

_____

_____

What was most surprising or interesting to you about this selection?

_____

_____

5 | Coping with an Aggressive Dog

by Michael W. Fox

Do you know what to do if you find yourself face-to-face with an unfriendly dog? Following the advice given in this selection could help you get out of a bad situation safely.

We all, sooner or later, encounter mean dogs. There is no set way for handling the situation. Each dog is different. But all dogs tend to conform to certain predictable rules of behavior. When you find yourself face-to-face with an aggressive animal, knowing these rules can help you avoid trouble. Here are some general words of advice:

1. *Never stare at a dog.* Staring is a threat. A dog may read a stare as a challenge and attack you.

2. *Never run or walk quickly past—or away from—a strange dog.* Your flight may release the dog's chase response, and you may get bitten. Always pass a dog slowly, even backwards (facing the animal) if you believe it may chase you when you leave its territory. (Its territory includes its house, yard, and part of the street.)

3. *Try to avoid showing your fear. Keep calm.* A dog can read fear in your eyes and body movements. Whistle, walk slowly, speak in a firm and confident voice. You might say, for example, "Good dog, I'm your friend," or "Good dog, why don't you go home?"

4. *Remember that even friendly dogs will bark at you.* It is their job to defend their territory, and you may be intruding. Talk to the dog, and smile if it wags its tail and doesn't snarl or put up the hair on its back. Stand still and call it to you. The dog may want to be friends. If it approaches in a friendly way, stand still so it can sniff you. That's good manners. Then bend or squat down, and let it sniff your hand.

If you have a newspaper route or other delivery job, take cookies or dog biscuits with you. Any dog you may fear could become one of your regular canine buddies if it's waiting for a treat from you each time. One dog named Bruce used to wait for me on my paper route; after I got to his house, he would tag along on the rest of my deliveries.

If you do get a buddy dog, watch out for traffic. Some dogs have no traffic sense and shouldn't be encouraged to enter the street.

5. *Observe how a strange dog reacts to you as you approach it slowly.* If the dog's in its own territory, it will probably bark at you. If it stays still, backs off, or comes toward you with its tail wagging in a low position, the dog is not likely to bite, even though it keeps barking.

If the dog stiffens, holds its head high, snarls, and stares at you, be careful. If it lowers its head as though ready to charge, or is snarling and showing its teeth, don't go any closer.

6. *As you leave the dog's territory, remember the golden rule of "cool." Don't turn and run; back away slowly, keeping the dog in view all the time.* Remember, since many people get bitten as they are *leaving* a dog's territory, the dog may read it as weakness or submission if you turn your back and walk away. If a dog seems to be after you, face up to it and stand your ground. Call out to its owners, and shout in a powerful, angry voice: "No, boy, down. Go home!" This may be enough bluff to scare the dog away.

Never lean back. Any backward movement appears to the dog as fear. Keep your weight forward. If the dog jumps at you, you'll be ready. An upward thrust of your knee into the dog's chest and a faceful of your jacket sleeve will deter many dogs.

7. *Dogs rarely attack, so don't start worrying and acting scared around any dog.* Most dogs are like you and me. They're scared about getting into a fight, but they sometimes like to act tough, especially around their own block. Don't ignore dogs you meet; that might make them suspicious. Say, "Hi, dog, how are you today?" If you act friendly and confident, the dog won't be scared and will be less likely to challenge you.

9. *Never try to forcibly make friends with a strange dog. Let it come to you.* There's nothing wrong with you if you like dogs but some seem to bark at you and hate you anyway. They may be scared or putting on a show because you're a stranger, trying to drive you away from their territory.

Let me encourage you to get to know and enjoy the friendly and curious dogs that you meet. ∎

✔ Enter your reading time below. Then look up your reading speed on the Words-per-Minute table on page 130.

Reading Time _____

Reading Speed _____

Enter your reading speed on the Reading Speed graph on page 131.

Comprehension

Put an **X** in the box next to the correct answer for each question or statement. Do not look back at the selection.

1. Why shouldn't you stare at a dog?
   - ☐ a. The dog may feel threatened.
   - ☐ b. The dog may feel frightened.
   - ☐ c. The dog may run away.

2. Even friendly dogs will bark at you if they think you
   - ☐ a. will hurt them.
   - ☐ b. have some food.
   - ☐ c. are intruding into their territory.

3. The author suggests taking cookies or biscuits on a delivery job to
   - ☐ a. help make friends with any dog you meet.
   - ☐ b. eat when you get hungry.
   - ☐ c. throw at any dogs that might attack you.

4. If a dog approaches in a friendly way, you should
   - ☐ a. pat the dog's head.
   - ☐ b. stand still, and let it sniff you.
   - ☐ c. walk slowly away.

5. A dog is not likely to bite if
   - ☐ a. it snarls and shows its teeth.
   - ☐ b. its tail is wagging in a low position.
   - ☐ c. it stiffens, holds its head high, and stares at you.

6. The author says you shouldn't ignore dogs because
   - ☐ a. you may hurt their feelings.
   - ☐ b. they might go away.
   - ☐ c. they might get suspicious.

7. What movement appears to the dog as fear?
   - ☐ a. leaning forward
   - ☐ b. leaning back
   - ☐ c. bending or squatting down

8. What should you do if a dog attacks you?
   - ☐ a. run away
   - ☐ b. stand perfectly still
   - ☐ c. face up to it

✎ _____ Number of correct answers
Enter this number on the Comprehension
graph on page 132.

Critical Thinking

Put an **X** in the box next to the best answer
for each question or statement. You may look
back at the selection if you'd like.

1. If dogs rarely attack, why did the author
   write this piece?
   - ☐ a. to make you afraid of dogs
   - ☐ b. to advise you on how to handle the
     few dogs that might attack
   - ☐ c. to encourage you to make friends
     with dogs

2. Which of the following statements best
   expresses the main idea of the selection?
   - ☐ a. Sooner or later, everyone
     encounters mean dogs.
   - ☐ b. Dogs rarely attack, so you shouldn't
     worry and act strangely around
     dogs.
   - ☐ c. All dogs tend to conform to certain
     predictable rules of behavior, and
     knowing these rules can help you
     avoid trouble.

3. Why shouldn't you try to force a dog to be
   friends?
   - ☐ a. Most dogs are dangerous.
   - ☐ b. Some dogs don't like to make
     friends.
   - ☐ c. Some dogs carry diseases.

4. Based on what you read, you can predict
   that when you enter a strange dog's
   territory, it almost always will
   - ☐ a. attack you.
   - ☐ b. bark at you.
   - ☐ c. wag its tail.

5. Why should you never turn your back and
   walk away when leaving a strange dog's
   territory?
   - ☐ a. The dog may read it as a weakness
     and attack.
   - ☐ b. The dog's feelings may be hurt.
   - ☐ c. You would not see the dog coming
     if it were to attack.

6. Which of the following is a statement of
   opinion rather than fact?
   - ☐ a. All dogs tend to conform to certain
     predictable rules of behavior.
   - ☐ b. A dog may read a stare as a
     challenge and attack you.
   - ☐ c. We all, sooner or later, encounter
     mean dogs.

7. Which phrase best describes "traffic
   sense"?
   - ☐ a. awareness of where you parked
   - ☐ b. awareness of oncoming cars
   - ☐ c. awareness of how to drive

8. Which statement does not give good
   advice about how to act when meeting a
   strange dog?
   - ☐ a. Turn your back and quickly move
     away.
   - ☐ b. Pass the dog slowly, always facing
     the animal.
   - ☐ c. Talk to the dog, and smile if it wags
     its tail and doesn't snarl.

✎ _____ Number of correct answers
Enter this number on the Critical Thinking
graph on page 133.

Vocabulary

Each numbered sentence contains an underlined word from the selection. Following are three definitions. Put an **X** in the box next to the best meaning of the word as it is used in the sentence.

1. We all, sooner or later, <u>encounter</u> mean dogs.
   - ☐ a. make
   - ☐ b. meet
   - ☐ c. hurt

2. When you find yourself face-to-face with an <u>aggressive</u> animal, knowing these rules can help you avoid trouble.
   - ☐ a. barking
   - ☐ b. bold
   - ☐ c. strange

3. Your <u>flight</u> may release the dog's chase response, and you may get bitten.
   - ☐ a. fear
   - ☐ b. appearance
   - ☐ c. retreat

4. It is their job to defend their territory, and you may be <u>intruding</u>.
   - ☐ a. leaving without permission
   - ☐ b. entering without permission
   - ☐ c. entering with permission

5. Any dog you may fear could become one of your regular <u>canine</u> buddies.
   - ☐ a. dog
   - ☐ b. hungry
   - ☐ c. friendly

6. Observe how a strange dog <u>reacts</u> to you as you approach it slowly.
   - ☐ a. retreats
   - ☐ b. snarls
   - ☐ c. responds

7. Don't ignore dogs you meet; that might make them <u>suspicious</u>.
   - ☐ a. think nothing is wrong
   - ☐ b. think you are angry
   - ☐ c. think something is wrong

8. Never try to <u>forcibly</u> make friends with a strange dog.
   - ☐ a. repeatedly
   - ☐ b. falsely
   - ☐ c. strongly

✎ _____ **Number of correct answers**
Enter this number on the Vocabulary graph on page 134.

Personal Response

Have you or anyone you know ever encountered an aggressive animal? Describe the situation.

_____

_____

Do you think all dogs should be restrained, or should they be allowed to run free? Explain your answer.

_____

_____

6 | The Phantom Tollbooth

by Norton Juster

The Phantom Tollbooth is the story of Milo, a bored boy, who assembles a genuine turnpike tollbooth in his room. After depositing a coin and going through the tollbooth, he suddenly finds himself in a very strange land. In this passage from the book, Milo finds himself stuck in the Doldrums.

Milo said, quite indignantly, "Everybody thinks."

"We don't," shouted the Lethargarians all at once.

"And most of the time *you* don't," said a yellow one sitting in a daffodil. "That's why you're here. You weren't thinking, and you weren't paying attention either. People who don't pay attention often get stuck in the Doldrums." And with that he toppled out of the flower and fell snoring into the grass.

Milo couldn't help laughing at the little creature's strange behavior.

"Stop that at once," ordered the plaid one clinging to his stocking. "Laughing is against the law. Don't you have a rule book? It's local ordinance 574381-W."

Milo found Ordinance 574381-W: "In the Doldrums, laughter is frowned upon and smiling is permitted only on alternate Thursdays. Violators shall be dealt with most harshly."

"Well, if you can't laugh or think, what can you do?" asked Milo.

"Anything as long as it's nothing, and everything as long as it isn't anything," explained another. "There's lots to do; we have a very busy schedule—

"At 8 o'clock we get up, and then we spend "From 8 to 9 daydreaming.

"From 9 to 9:30 we take our early midmorning nap.

"From 9:30 to 10:30 we dawdle and delay.

"From 10:30 to 11:30 we take our late early morning nap.

"From 11 to 12 we bide our time and then eat lunch.

"From 1 to 2 we linger and loiter.

"From 2 to 2:30 we take our early afternoon nap.

"From 2:30 to 3:30 we put off for tomorrow what we could have done today.

"From 3:30 to 4 we take our early late afternoon nap.

"From 4 to 5 we loaf and lounge until dinner.

"From 7 to 8 we take our early evening nap, and then for an hour before we go to bed at 9 o'clock we waste time.

"As you can see, that leaves almost no time for brooding, lagging, plodding, or procrastinating, and if we stopped to think or laugh, we'd never get nothing done."

"You mean you'd never get anything done," corrected Milo.

"We don't want to get anything done," snapped another angrily; "we want to get nothing done."

"You see," continued another in a more conciliatory tone, "it's really quite strenuous doing nothing all day, so once a week we take a holiday and go nowhere, which was just where we were going when you came along. Would you care to join us?"

"I might as well," thought Milo; "that's where I seem to be going anyway."

"Tell me," he yawned, for he felt ready

for a nap now himself, "does everyone here do nothing?"

"Everyone but the terrible watchdog," said two of them, shuddering in chorus. "He's always sniffing around to see that nobody wastes time. A most unpleasant character."

"The watchdog?" Milo said quizzically.

"THE WATCHDOG," shouted another, fainting from fright, for racing down the road barking furiously and kicking up a great cloud of dust was the very dog of whom they had been speaking.

"RUN!"

"WAKE UP!"

"RUN!"

"HERE HE COMES!"

"THE WATCHDOG!"

Great shouts filled the air as the Lethargarians scattered in all directions and soon disappeared entirely.

"R-R-R-G-H-R-O-R-R-H-F-F," exclaimed the watchdog as he dashed up to the car, loudly puffing and panting.

Milo's eyes opened wide, for there in front of him was a large dog with a perfectly normal head, four feet, and a tail—and the body of a loudly ticking alarm clock.

"What are you doing here?" growled the watchdog.

"Just killing time," replied Milo apologetically. "You see—"

"KILLING TIME!" roared the dog—so furiously that his alarm went off. "It's bad enough wasting time without killing it." And he shuddered at the thought. "Why are you in the Doldrums anyway—don't you have anywhere to go?"

"I was on my way to Dictionopolis when I got stuck here," explained Milo. "Can you help me?"

"Help you! You must help yourself," the dog replied, carefully winding himself with

his left hind leg. "I suppose you know why you got stuck."

"I guess I just wasn't thinking," said Milo.

"PRECISELY," shouted the dog as his alarm went off again. "Now you know what you must do."

"I'm afraid I don't," admitted Milo, feeling quite stupid.

"Well," continued the watchdog impatiently, "since you got here by not thinking, it seems reasonable to expect that, in order to get out, you must start thinking." And with that he hopped into the car. ∎

✔ Enter your reading time below. Then look up your reading speed on the Words-per-Minute table on page 130.

Reading Time   _____

Reading Speed   _____

Enter your reading speed on the Reading Speed graph on page 131.

Comprehension

Put an ✘ in the box next to the correct answer for each question or statement. Do not look back at the selection.

1. Where does Milo find himself?
   - ☐ a. Dictionopolis
   - ☐ b. the Doldrums
   - ☐ c. Lethargar

2. What do the Lethargarians do all day?
   - ☐ a. think
   - ☐ b. everything
   - ☐ c. nothing

3. What did the law, Ordinance 574381-W, prohibit?
   - ☐ a. thinking
   - ☐ b. laughing
   - ☐ c. working

4. The Lethargarians found that following their busy schedule was quite
   - [ ] a. strenuous.
   - [ ] b. restful.
   - [ ] c. boring.

5. The Lethargarians felt the need to take a holiday once a
   - [ ] a. month.
   - [ ] b. week.
   - [ ] c. year.

6. Where did the Lethargarians go on their holiday?
   - [ ] a. Dictionopolis
   - [ ] b. everywhere
   - [ ] c. nowhere

7. The watchdog became upset with Milo when Milo told him he was
   - [ ] a. killing time.
   - [ ] b. wasting time.
   - [ ] c. saving time.

8. Milo arrived in the Doldrums because he was
   - [ ] a. not thinking.
   - [ ] b. thinking too hard.
   - [ ] c. trying to get there.

✎ _____ Number of correct answers
Enter this number on the Comprehension graph on page 132.

Critical Thinking

Put an **X** in the box next to the best answer for each question or statement. You may look back at the selection if you'd like.

1. The author intended this story to be
   - [ ] a. humorous.
   - [ ] b. serious.
   - [ ] c. scary.

2. Who is the narrator of this story?
   - [ ] a. Milo
   - [ ] b. a Lethargarian
   - [ ] c. an outside observer

3. The watchdog has a clock for a body because he
   - [ ] a. needs to stay awake.
   - [ ] b. represents order.
   - [ ] c. keeps running down

4. The Lethargarians can best be described as
   - [ ] a. lazy.
   - [ ] b. peaceful.
   - [ ] c. fearful.

5. What will happen if Milo doesn't start thinking?
   - [ ] a. The watchdog will bite him.
   - [ ] b. He won't get out of the Doldrums.
   - [ ] c. The Lethargarians will kick him out of the Doldrums.

6. Which of the following is a statement of opinion rather than fact?
   - [ ] a. "I was on my way to Dictionopolis when I got stuck here."
   - [ ] b. "It's bad enough wasting time, without killing it."
   - [ ] c. "Laughing is against the law."

7. Where was Milo going before he got stuck with the Lethargarians?
   - [ ] a. to the Doldrums
   - [ ] b. to see the watchdog
   - [ ] c. to Dictionopolis

8. Milo's attitude toward the Lethargarians can best be described as
   - ☐ a. envious.
   - ☐ b. friendly.
   - ☐ c. suspicious.

✎ _____ Number of correct answers
Enter this number on the Critical Thinking graph on page 133.

Vocabulary

Each numbered sentence contains an underlined word or phrase from the selection. Following are three definitions. Put an ✗ in the box next to the best meaning of the word as it is used in the sentence.

1. And with that he <u>toppled</u> out of the flower and fell snoring into the grass.
   - ☐ a. tumbled
   - ☐ b. jumped
   - ☐ c. flew

2. Laughter is frowned upon and smiling is <u>permitted</u> only on alternate Thursdays."
   - ☐ a. forbidden
   - ☐ b. encouraged
   - ☐ c. allowed

3. "It's really quite <u>strenuous</u> doing nothing all day."
   - ☐ a. easy
   - ☐ b. fun
   - ☐ c. hard

4. "As you can see, that leaves almost no time for brooding, lagging, plodding, or <u>procrastinating</u>."
   - ☐ a. speeding
   - ☐ b. delaying
   - ☐ c. chatting

5. "Everyone but the terrible watchdog," said two of them, shuddering <u>in chorus</u>.
   - ☐ a. together
   - ☐ b. separately
   - ☐ c. one after the other

6. "KILLING TIME!" roared the dog—so <u>furiously</u> that his alarm went off.
   - ☐ a. happily
   - ☐ b. angrily
   - ☐ c. swift

7. "<u>PRECISELY</u>," shouted the dog as his alarm went off again.
   - ☐ a. exactly
   - ☐ b. preposterous
   - ☐ c. ridiculous

8. "Well," continued the watchdog <u>impatiently</u>, "since you got here by not thinking, it seems that in order to get out, you must start thinking."
   - ☐ a. slowly and calmly
   - ☐ b. quickly and crossly
   - ☐ c. with patience

✎ _____ Number of correct answers
Enter this number on the Vocabulary graph on page 134.

Personal Response

Laughing was against the law in the Doldrums. Imagine and then describe an equally strange law that Milo might encounter in Dictionopolis.

_____

_____

_____

7 | Black Holes

by Henry and Melissa Billings

Scientists can't see them, but they are pretty certain they exist somewhere out in deep space. They are black holes, the fantastic mystery of outer space.

It was a star vastly larger than our own sun. For hundreds of years this giant star burned brightly in its corner of the universe. Then, at the end of its life span, a bizarre thing happened. The dying star began to collapse in on itself. While the star was in its death throes, all the matter that made up the star was squeezed together into a smaller and smaller area. Soon the star measured no more than a mile across. Its matter was so tightly packed that a chunk of it the size of a small marble weighed as much as a mountain.

As the dead star continued to fall into itself, it brought with it every bit of matter in the area. Every speck of dust, every stray atom, was dragged into it. The star had become a black hole. A black hole is a small area of matter so dense that not even a light beam can escape the pull of its gravity.

Since no light can leave black holes, there is no way for us to see them. They are invisible. We know of their existence because of the strange things that happen around them. Light that is traveling through space just vanishes.

Just how wild is a black hole? Let's take a look at gravity. A common expression related to gravity is, "What goes up must come down." When someone throws a ball into the air, it must return to Earth. This happens because Earth attracts the ball, or pulls it toward itself. A flowerpot that is knocked off a third-story ledge will always hit the sidewalk. It is only the great thrust of giant rockets that allows the space shuttle to escape the pull of Earth's gravity.

On a planet with double or triple Earth's gravity, objects would act quite differently, because the pull, or attraction, would be much stronger. A ball thrown into the air would not go very high, and it would plunge quickly back to the surface of the planet. A falling flowerpot would be a lethal weapon. It would kill any luckless pedestrian who might happen to get hit by it. Rockets far more powerful than those used on Earth would be needed to break away from the pull of the planet's gravity.

Beams of light, however, would have no trouble at all escaping from this planet. Even if the force of gravity were increased to a million times that of Earth, light beams would still not be affected. Humans on such a world, though, would be crushed flatter than their own shadows.

Only if the amount of gravity were many billions of times stronger than Earth's would light beams bend back to the surface. That is the case with a black hole. It is hard to imagine just how dense and heavy black hole matter is. A penny made from black hole matter would rip through your pocket and plunge through the earth with the greatest of ease. When it emerged on the other side, it would hover in the air for a moment and then plunge back through the earth.

Black holes are the most bizarre objects in the universe. Nothing ever leaves a black hole. No light leaves it. No physical objects leave it. Once something enters a black hole, it is there forever. Black holes are like permanent detention halls in the sky. If a travel agent were to arrange a flight to a black hole, it would have to be a one-way trip. As the scientist Robert Jastrow said, "It is almost as though the material inside the black hole no longer belongs to our universe."

Suppose, just for the sake of amusement, that you happened to drop into a black hole. What would happen to you? Think of going feet first. Your feet would be pulled down faster than your ears. As a result, you would be drawn into a very thin strand of matter. Then the individual atoms in your body would be pulled apart.

Were you to survive the trip, however, some scientists believe that you would emerge in the fourth dimension. You would be in a totally different universe. The point where matter exits from this universe and goes into the next is referred to as a white hole. Many scientists believe that there are at least five black holes in our section of the universe. But, then, no one really knows for sure. Our knowledge of black holes is based only on informed guesswork. ■

✔ Enter your reading time below. Then look up your reading speed on the Words-per-Minute table on page 130.

Reading Time _____

Reading Speed _____

Enter your reading speed on the Reading Speed graph on page 131.

Comprehension

Put an **X** in the box next to the correct answer for each question or statement. Do not look back at the selection.

1. Gravity in a black hole is
   □ a. so great that even light can't escape.
   □ b. twice that of Earth.
   □ c. 100 times that of Earth.

2. A black hole is best described as a
   □ a. small area of dense matter located in outer space.
   □ b. huge area in outer space containing loose dust particles and stray atoms.
   □ c. large hole in outer space opening into the fourth dimension.

3. We cannot see black holes because they are
   □ a. too far away to be seen through telescopes.
   □ b. invisible, since no light can leave them.
   □ c. hidden behind other stars.

4. Black hole matter the size of a marble
   □ a. would sink several feet into the ground.
   □ b. would need a large crane to lift it.
   □ c. weighs as much as a mountain.

5. On a planet with double Earth's gravity, a ball thrown into the air would fall back to the planet's surface
   □ a. in about the same time it would on Earth.
   □ b. more slowly that it would on Earth.
   □ c. more quickly than it would on Earth.

6. What is a white hole?
   □ a. the point where matter exits from this universe into the next
   □ b. the bottom of a black hole
   □ c. a hole similar to a black hole except that it allows light to escape

7. Scientists believe that in our section of the universe there are at least
   □ a. ten black holes.
   □ b. five black holes.
   □ c. two black holes.

8. Scientists' knowledge of black holes is based on
   ☐ a. proven facts.
   ☐ b. informed guesswork.
   ☐ c. exploration by space satellites.

✎ _____ Number of correct answers
Enter this number on the Comprehension graph on page 132.

Critical Thinking

Put an **X** in the box next to the best answer for each question or statement. You may look back at the selection if you'd like.

1. The authors use the first sentence of the selection to
   ☐ a. inform you that our sun is a star.
   ☐ b. compare a star to our own sun.
   ☐ c. tell you the size of our sun.

2. Which of the following statements best expresses the main idea of the selection?
   ☐ a. No one has actually seen a black hole because no light can escape from one.
   ☐ b. Black holes are strange, extremely dense objects, whose existence scientists can only guess about.
   ☐ c. Outer space is filled with strange and wonderful phenomena that scientists do not fully understand.

3. Based on what you read, you can conclude that
   ☐ a. light is the last thing affected by the pull of gravity.
   ☐ b. one day Earth will become a black hole.
   ☐ c. scientists now have a complete understanding of black holes.

4. From the selection, you can predict that if a spaceship suddenly encountered a black hole in outer space the passengers would
   ☐ a. enter a totally different universe.
   ☐ b. be lost forever in space.
   ☐ c. be killed instantly.

5. A black hole results from
   ☐ a. a collision of two giant asteroids.
   ☐ b. the death of a giant star.
   ☐ c. the explosion of a sun like our own.

6. Which of the following is a statement of opinion rather than fact?
   ☐ a. Our knowledge of black holes is based on informed guesswork.
   ☐ b. It is only the great thrust of giant rockets that allows the space shuttle to escape the pull of Earth's gravity.
   ☐ c. Black holes are the most bizarre objects in the universe.

7. What causes a ball thrown into the air to fall back to the ground?
   ☐ a. A black hole pulls the object back to Earth.
   ☐ b. A white hole pulls the object back to Earth.
   ☐ c. Gravity pulls the object back to Earth.

8. Which of the following best describes what scientists consider black holes to be?
   ☐ a. a deadly threat
   ☐ b. a mystery
   ☐ c. bizarre objects

✎ _____ Number of correct answers
Enter this number on the Critical Thinking graph on page 133.

Vocabulary

Each numbered sentence contains an underlined word from the selection. Following are three definitions. Put an ✗ in the box next to the best meaning of the word as it is used in the sentence.

1. Then, at the end of its life span, a <u>bizarre</u> thing happened.
   - ☐ a. comical
   - ☐ b. ordinary
   - ☐ c. weird

2. A black hole is a small area of matter so <u>dense</u> that not even a light beam can escape the pull of its gravity.
   - ☐ a. thin
   - ☐ b. thick
   - ☐ c. dark

3. We know of their <u>existence</u> because of the strange things that happen around them.
   - ☐ a. size
   - ☐ b. being
   - ☐ c. danger

4. It is only the great <u>thrust</u> of giant rockets that allows the space shuttle to escape the pull of Earth's gravity.
   - ☐ a. design
   - ☐ b. forward pull
   - ☐ c. rearward push

5. A ball thrown into the air would not go very high, and it would <u>plunge</u> quickly back to the surface of the planet.
   - ☐ a. dive
   - ☐ b. rise
   - ☐ c. float

6. A falling flowerpot would be a <u>lethal</u> weapon.
   - ☐ a. illegal
   - ☐ b. harmless
   - ☐ c. deadly

7. When it emerged on the other side, it would <u>hover</u> in the air for a moment and then plunge back through the earth.
   - ☐ a. sink below
   - ☐ b. float
   - ☐ c. explode

8. Were you to survive the trip, however, some scientists believe that you would <u>emerge</u> in the fourth dimension.
   - ☐ a. come out
   - ☐ b. go back
   - ☐ c. die

✎ _____ Number of correct answers
Enter this number on the Vocabulary graph on page 134.

Personal Response

What was most surprising or interesting to you about this selection?

_____

_____

One question I would like to ask the authors about black holes is

_____

_____

8 | The Trade

by David E. Griffith

This story is about Tim McCully, a boy who is having a rough time both on and off the baseball field. In this passage from the story, Tim meets a stranger.

Tim McCully stepped up to the plate, and the Rocket outfielders moved in so close they were practically chatting with the infielders. It was a challenge, and Tim McCully was fairly sure he couldn't meet it.

There were two outs, the tying run on third. The pitcher eyed Tim the way a hungry lizard watches a bug. He wound up and released.

The ball slapped the catcher's mitt with a dull thump.

"Steerike!"

"Don't worry," Coach Davis called from the Harkerton Hawks' dugout. "Next one's yours."

The words of encouragement only made Tim more nervous. His stomach turned to ice water, and his hands were so sweaty he feared he might drop the bat. *If I'm lucky*, he thought, *a fastball will knock me unconscious, and I won't wake up until the season is over.*

"Steerike two!"

Tim's mind began to wander. He thought about his older brother, Dan, and how he could have saved the day. He'd probably send one over the fence to win the game. *I'd give anything to be that good*, Tim thought. But it was useless to think about such things. He wasn't as good as his brother. Besides, Dan was. . .

The pitcher cut loose a fastball. Tim swung, made contact, but only managed a pop out to the pitcher.

After the teams shook hands, the Hawks milled around the dugout. Finally Gord Foster, the Hawks' pitcher, spoke to Tim. "We're going to Lloyd's for sodas. You interested?"

Tim shrugged. "Nah, I'm not really in the mood. I have to get home. Thanks."

But Tim didn't go home. He slumped against the backstop and stared at his baseball cap on the grass. The hat used to be Dan's.

Dan McCully died on a rainy day the year before. He was riding his bike home after a game when he lost control on the wet pavement. His head struck a curb. He was only 15 years old. Since then nothing had been the same. In two years Tim would be the same age as Dan had been.

Tim wanted to quit playing ball, but he knew it would disappoint his mom and dad. He buried his head in his arms.

"Tough game, son. Wouldn't blame a boy for quitting after something like that."

Tim nearly jumped out of his shirt. The voice seemed to have come from the dugout. He sidled over to the top step and peered in.

"I didn't mean to startle you," a white-haired man said. He was sitting in the middle of the bench, his long legs crossed at the ankles. Tim had never seen this man before.

"I've seen some tough moments in baseball," the man said, "and that was one of the roughest. I've also seen moments that make the diamond shine. I was in the crowd the day Babe Ruth knocked one out of the park for that sick boy."

Babe Ruth, Tim thought. *But he played in the 30s and 40s.*

The stranger shook his head and smacked his lips. "People see what they want. My name's Walker. My friends call me Satch." He extended a hand, and Tim stepped down into the dugout to introduce himself. Satch's hand was cold as clay.

"You could quit playing ball, son, but it would be a shame. You're a natural, and if anyone knows talent, it's Satch Walker. I've trained some of the greats. What do you say I give you some pointers?"

Tim's cheeks blushed. "I don't think so. Anyway, I don't have enough money for a private trainer."

Satch turned his head as if embarrassed. "Money doesn't interest me, boy. In fact, I'll give you a free tip right now, and if you don't improve by tomorrow, you'll never have to talk to me again."

"OK. What's the tip?"

"You need to get mean, boy. I look at you and see 75 pounds of *please* and *thank you*. That might work at Grandma's house, but it doesn't cut it on the field. When you see that pitch coming, think of it as someone who's done you wrong. Maybe a teacher who failed you, or a teammate who laughed when you missed a catch. You've got to reach down and pull some meanness out of yourself."

Tim was taken aback by Satch's remarks. He wasn't sure how to respond except to say thanks.

"Don't mention it, boy. Think it over, and maybe I'll see you tomorrow." Satch excused himself and shuffled into the gray evening, whistling an old tune. ∎

✔ Enter your reading time below. Then look up your reading speed on the Words-per-Minute table on page 130.

Reading Time _____

Reading Speed _____

Enter your reading speed on the Reading Speed graph on page 131.

Comprehension

Put an **X** in the box next to the correct answer for each question or statement. Do not look back at the selection,

1. For what team did Tim play?
   - ☐ a. the Rockets
   - ☐ b. the Hawks
   - ☐ c. the Braves

2. The author compares the opposing pitcher to a
   - ☐ a. hungry lizard.
   - ☐ b. circling hawk.
   - ☐ c. mean bulldog.

3. In his at bat with two out and the tying run at third, Tim
   - ☐ a. struck out.
   - ☐ b. popped out to the pitcher.
   - ☐ c. grounded weakly back to the pitcher.

4. What did Tim do right after the game?
   - ☐ a. He went to Lloyd's for sodas.
   - ☐ b. He went home.
   - ☐ c. He stayed at the ballpark.

5. Tim's brother, Dan, died in
   - ☐ a. an automobile accident.
   - ☐ b. a house fire.
   - ☐ c. a bicycle accident.

6. Where was the stranger when he first spoke to Tim?
   - ☐ a. in the grandstand
   - ☐ b. in the dugout
   - ☐ c. behind the backstop

7. What was the tip the stranger gave Tim?
   - ☐ a. to get mean
   - ☐ b. to practice harder
   - ☐ c. to learn how to pitch

8. The stranger made it clear to Tim that he was not interested in
   - ☐ a. giving him any more free tips.
   - ☐ b. seeing him again.
   - ☐ c. getting any money from him.

✎ _____ Number of correct answers
Enter this number on the Comprehension graph on page 132.

Critical Thinking

Put an **X** in the box next to the best answer for each question or statement. You may look back at the selection if you'd like.

1. What kind of mood or feeling does the author create in this story?
   - ☐ a. sad
   - ☐ b. peaceful
   - ☐ c. mysterious

2. Who is the narrator of this story?
   - ☐ a. Tim
   - ☐ b. the stranger
   - ☐ c. an outside observer

3. The best title for this passage from the story "The Trade" is
   - ☐ a. "A Tough Game for Tim"
   - ☐ b. "The Mysterious Stranger"
   - ☐ c. "Tim and His Brother"

4. Tim wanted to quit baseball because
   - ☐ a. he really didn't like baseball.
   - ☐ b. he was discouraged about his playing.
   - ☐ c. his teammates were giving him a hard time.

5. What caused Tim's mind to wander while he was at bat?
   - ☐ a. He was wishing he were somewhere else.
   - ☐ b. He was thinking of how he was embarrassing himself.
   - ☐ c. He was thinking about his older brother, Dan.

6. Which of the following is a statement of opinion rather than fact?
   - ☐ a. "I was in the crowd the day Babe Ruth knocked one out of the park for that sick boy."
   - ☐ b. "You need to get mean, boy."
   - ☐ c. "Anyway, I don't have enough money for a private trainer."

7. Compared to Tim McCully, Dan McCully
   - ☐ a. was a better athlete.
   - ☐ b. disliked sports.
   - ☐ c. was younger.

8. Based on this passage, you can predict that probably
   - ☐ a. the stranger will not return.
   - ☐ b. the stranger will return.
   - ☐ c. Tim will quit baseball.

✎ _____ Number of correct answers
Enter this number on the Critical Thinking graph on page 133.

Vocabulary

Each numbered sentence contains an underlined word or phrase from the selection. Following are three definitions. Put an ✗ in the box next to the best meaning of the word as it is used in the sentence.

1. Tim McCully stepped up to the plate, and the Rocket outfielders moved in so close they were practically <u>chatting</u> with the infielders.
   - ☐ a. talking
   - ☐ b. playing
   - ☐ c. relaxing

2. It was a <u>challenge</u>, and Tim McCully was fairly sure he couldn't meet it.
   - ☐ a. promise
   - ☐ b. insult
   - ☐ c. test

3. After the teams shook hands, the Hawks <u>milled around</u> the dugout.
   - ☐ a. sat around
   - ☐ b. jumped around
   - ☐ c. moved aimlessly around

4. Tim <u>shrugged</u>. "Nah, I'm not really in the mood."
   - ☐ a. folded his arms
   - ☐ b. raised his shoulders
   - ☐ c. stepped back

5. He <u>slumped</u> against the backstop and stared at his baseball cap on the grass.
   - ☐ a. pushed
   - ☐ b. leaned
   - ☐ c. dropped heavily

6. "I didn't mean to <u>startle</u> you," a white-haired man said.
   - ☐ a. frighten
   - ☐ b. stare at
   - ☐ c. bother

7. He <u>extended</u> a hand, and Tim stepped down into the dugout to introduce himself.
   - ☐ a. covered
   - ☐ b. stretched out
   - ☐ c. held back

8. He wasn't sure how to <u>respond</u> except to say thanks.
   - ☐ a. understand
   - ☐ b. apologize
   - ☐ c. answer

_____ Number of correct answers
Enter this number on the Vocabulary graph on page 134.

Personal Response

Who do you think the stranger is, and what do you think he really wants?

_____

_____

I know how Tim feels because

_____

_____

9 | Go for the Gold

Skiing down a mountain at speeds of more than 60 miles per hour takes great skill and courage for skiers with two legs. Imagine the amount of skill and courage such a feat would require for a person with only one leg.

Diana Golden was 12 years old when she found out she had cancer. She was walking home one day after playing in the snow when her right leg simply gave out. Doctors diagnosed the problem as bone cancer. They recommended amputating her leg above the knee.

When Diana heard the news, she asked the first question that popped into her mind: "Will I still be able to ski?"

"When the doctors said yes," she later recalled, "I figured it wouldn't be too bad."

That attitude typified Diana's outlook on life. Losing a leg would devastate most children, but Diana refused to dwell on the negative. "Losing a leg?" she'd say. "It's nothing. A body part."

Most of all, Diana didn't want to let cancer stop her from doing what she loved. And what she loved was skiing. Diana had been on skis since the age of five. Her home in Lincoln, Massachusetts, was just a couple of hours from New Hampshire's Cannon Mountain. After the amputation, Diana worked hard to get back to the mountain. "I always skied, and I intended to keep on skiing. There was never any question in my mind about that," she declared. Seven months after losing her leg, Diana met her goal. She was back out on the slopes.

Skiing wasn't quite the same with just one leg, but Diana made the best of it. She used outriggers—special ski poles that were like crutches with small skis attached. She learned to go faster on one leg than most people could go on two. In high school, Diana became a member of her school's ski racing team. And in 1979, when she was just 17, she earned a spot on the U.S. Disabled Ski Team.

After high school, Diana Golden went on to Dartmouth College. There she saw how top two-legged skiers trained. Determined not to be left behind, Diana began training with the Dartmouth team. When they ran around the track, she followed them on crutches. When they ran up and down the steps of the football stadium, she went up and down the steps too—by hopping. "I had to adapt," she later explained. "I was an athlete. I had one leg, which meant I had to do it differently."

In 1982, Diana entered her first international ski race. She went to the World Handicapped Championships in Norway, where she won the downhill competition.

Diana didn't just want to be a top disabled skier. She wanted to be a top skier, period. She wanted to prove herself against racers with two legs, not just those with one. In order to be the best, Diana had to give up her outriggers. She taught herself to ski with regular ski poles. That meant learning a new way of balancing herself. It also meant lifting lots of weights to strengthen her stomach, arms, and leg. With regular poles, she was able to reach speeds of 65 miles per hour.

Meanwhile, Diana still competed in ski races for the disabled. In fact, within a year of returning to the sport, she won gold medals in four big international races. But she also skied against nondisabled athletes. She lobbied to get the United States Ski Association (USSA) to welcome disabled skiers into its regular races.

Her efforts led to passage of the USSA "Golden Rule." This rule reserved slots for top disabled skiers early in a race. No longer would Diana and other disabled skiers have to wait until the end of the day to make their runs. That way they could ski the course before it became too rough.

In 1986, Diana won the Beck Award, which is given to the best American racer in international skiing. The next year, she placed 10th in a race against some of the best nondisabled skiers in the country. And in 1988, she was named *Ski Racing* magazine's U.S. Female Alpine Skier of the Year.

One of Diana's biggest thrills came in 1988. That was the year she went to the Olympic Games. Diana won the gold medal in the disabled giant slalom event. The U.S. Olympic Committee named her its Female Skier of the Year.

As a result of her courage and determination, Diana has changed the way the world looks at disabled athletes. People have begun to see them as strong and competent. "Everyone has some kind of 'disability,'" Diana says. "It's what we do with our abilities that matters."

In 1990, Diana retired from racing for good. ■

✔ Enter your reading time below. Then look up your reading speed on the Words-per-Minute table on page 130.

Reading Time _____

Reading Speed _____

Enter your reading speed on the Reading Speed graph on page 131.

Comprehension

Put an **X** in the box next to the correct answer for each question or statement. Do not look back at the selection.

1. Diana Golden found out she had cancer when she was
   - ☐ a. 5 years old.
   - ☐ b. 12 years old.
   - ☐ c. 17 years old.

2. After having her leg amputated, Diana was back skiing in
   - ☐ a. a year.
   - ☐ b. nine months.
   - ☐ c. seven months.

3. Diana learned to ski on one leg, using
   - ☐ a. regular ski poles.
   - ☐ b. outriggers.
   - ☐ c. crutches.

4. Diana earned a spot on the U.S. Disabled Ski Team when she was
   - ☐ a. at Dartmouth College.
   - ☐ b. in junior high school.
   - ☐ c. in high school.

5. How did passage of the "Golden Rule" by the U.S. Ski Association help disabled skiers?
   - ☐ a. It allowed disabled skiers to ski the course early in the race before it became too rough.
   - ☐ b. It allowed disabled skiers to have their own races, separate from nondisabled skiers.
   - ☐ c. It allowed disabled skiers to get a head start when racing against nondisabled skiers.

6. In 1986, Diana won the Beck Award, which is given to the best American
   - ☐ a. disabled skier.
   - ☐ b. woman skier.
   - ☐ c. racer in international skiing.

7. Diana was named the Female Skier of the Year the year she won
   - ☐ a. the Beck Award.
   - ☐ b. an Olympic gold medal.
   - ☐ c. her first international ski race.

8. In 1990, Diana
   - ☐ a. won her last race.
   - ☐ b. quit skiing for good.
   - ☐ c. retired from racing.

✎ _____ Number of correct answers
Enter this number on the Comprehension graph on page 132.

Critical Thinking

Put an ✗ in the box next to the best answer for each question or statement. You may look back at the selection if you'd like.

1. The author probably wrote this selection to
   - ☐ a. inform you about disabled skiers.
   - ☐ b. inspire you with Diana's courage.
   - ☐ c. describe the events in international ski competition.

2. Which of the following statements best expresses the main idea of the selection?
   - ☐ a. After losing a leg to cancer, Diana Golden became a champion skier in both disabled and nondisabled events.
   - ☐ b. Doctor's amputated Diana Golden's leg after they discovered she had bone cancer.
   - ☐ c. Diana Golden is one of the greatest skiers the United States has ever produced.

3. Based on what you've read, you can conclude that
   - ☐ a. Diana loved to compete.
   - ☐ b. Diana was content to be a top disabled skier.
   - ☐ c. Disabled skiers were not as athletic as nondisabled skiers.

4. Based on what Diana has said, you can predict that she
   - ☐ a. will never ski again.
   - ☐ b. will begin training so that she can compete in another sport.
   - ☐ c. will continue to face obstacles in her life with courage.

5. It is a disadvantage for ski racers to make their runs at the end of the day rather than early because
   - ☐ a. it's harder to see then.
   - ☐ b. the weather gets colder then.
   - ☐ c. the course is rough then.

6. Which of the following is a statement of opinion rather than fact?
   - ☐ a. "It's what we do with our abilities that matters."
   - ☐ b. After high school, Diana Golden went on to Dartmouth College.
   - ☐ c. In 1982, Diana entered her first international ski race.

7. Which of the following is the best summary of the selection?
   - ☐ a. After Diana Golden lost a leg to cancer, she learned to ski on one leg.
   - ☐ b. After losing a leg to cancer, Diana Golden worked hard to become a champion skier and a respected athlete.
   - ☐ c. After losing a leg to cancer, Diana Golden worked hard and was rewarded by winning an Olympic gold medal.

8. Which sentence below correctly restates the following: "Determined not to be left behind, Diana began training with the Dartmouth team."
   - [ ] a. Diana began training so she could make the Dartmouth team.
   - [ ] b. Diana trained with Dartmouth so she wouldn't finish last in her races.
   - [ ] c. Diana wanted to keep up, so she trained with the Dartmouth team.

✎ _____ Number of correct answers
Enter this number on the Critical Thinking graph on page 133.

Vocabulary

Each numbered sentence contains an underlined word from the selection. Following are three definitions. Put an **X** in the box next to the best meaning of the word as it is used in the sentence.

1. Doctors <u>diagnosed</u> the problem.
   - [ ] a. displayed
   - [ ] b. discussed
   - [ ] c. identified

2. They <u>recommended</u> amputating her leg.
   - [ ] a. decided against
   - [ ] b. suggested strongly
   - [ ] c. prevented

3. Losing a leg would <u>devastate</u> most children.
   - [ ] a. bother
   - [ ] b. overwhelm
   - [ ] c. encourage

4. "I had to <u>adapt</u>," she later explained.
   - [ ] a. fight hard
   - [ ] b. make some adjustments
   - [ ] c. refuse to change

5. She <u>lobbied</u> to get the United States Ski Association (USSA) to welcome disabled skiers into its regular races.
   - [ ] a. did not act
   - [ ] b. used her influence
   - [ ] c. voted

6. This rule <u>reserved</u> slots for top disabled skiers early in a race.
   - [ ] a. saved
   - [ ] b. took away
   - [ ] c. considered

7. People have begun to see them as strong and <u>competent</u>.
   - [ ] a. powerful
   - [ ] b. unfit
   - [ ] c. well-qualified

8. In 1990, Diana <u>retired</u> from racing.
   - [ ] a. withdrew
   - [ ] b. was forced
   - [ ] c. became tired

✎ _____ Number of correct answers
Enter this number on the Vocabulary graph on page 134.

Personal Response

Skiing was very important to Diana Golden. Describe an activity that is meaningful to you.

_____

_____

10 Just the Beginning

by Betty Miles

Just the thought of preparing for the many changes to come in high school can make eighth grade difficult enough. In this passage Cathy must also deal with some personal problems.

When you've been absent from school, you're supposed to bring an excuse from home to the office. It seemed as though I ought to have a note this time, too: "Please excuse Cathy for being absent. She was suspended." But no one expected a note. In a way, the whole suspension thing didn't seem so well organized. Nobody really talked to us when it happened, except Mrs. Vogel. And there was nobody to talk to after it was over.

I walked in the school door and went past the office to my locker, same as always. School was the same, too. A hall aide was standing next to my locker holding a baseball glove and arguing with two boys who had been playing catch with it in the hall. People were banging locker doors and calling to their friends. I looked up and saw Karen.

"Hi! How did you like suspension?" I asked.

"Listen, guess what?" she said. "I *am* going to go to boarding school next year."

"Really?"

"Yeah. I went with Mom on Friday to talk to people from this one school in Connecticut. It sounds neat. There's only sixty kids in the whole school, and you can have your own horse and keep him in a barn there."

"Do you think you'll go there?" I asked. I hadn't expected Karen to decide so fast. I was surprised. In a way, my feelings were hurt.

"I don't know. Mom wants me to look at some other schools. But I'm definitely going to go to boarding school somewhere. Mom says Camden High isn't the greatest if you want to get into a good college."

"Well, it's good enough for Julia," I said, feeling scared that maybe it wasn't. Julia still hadn't heard from any college.

"Oh, sure, I didn't mean Julia," Karen said quickly. "But for someone like me."

Or me, I thought. All I have on my record is ordinary grades. And a suspension.

The bell rang and we went on to Mrs. Inman's class. So many things were happening. Suspension was over. School was going to be over soon—only eight weeks to go. Julia would be graduating. Next year I'd be in ninth grade, and Karen would be away at boarding school. A lot of changes. I wasn't sure I was ready.

Mrs. Inman smiled at us. "Hello, girls. I see in the teachers' announcements that you were suspended last week. How in the world did that happen?"

"They canceled our gym class, and we went to The Break," I said.

"That doesn't seem so terrible," said Mrs. Inman. "But there *is* a rule and if you get caught, that's it."

"It's funny, though," I said. "Nobody even talked with us about it. They just sent letters to our parents."

"How did you spend the time?" Mrs. Inman asked.

"Cleaned my house and helped my father paint his store," I said. "It wasn't bad."

"I went for an interview at a boarding school," Karen said.

"Oh? How was it?"

"I liked it," Karen said. "Anyway, I'm going

to go away to some school next year."

"In a way I'm sorry to hear that," Mrs. Inman said. "I always think one of the good things about Camden is the mixture of people who go to it. I would hate to see the kids from wealthy families leave."

Mrs. Inman is so frank! I don't know anyone else who would just come out and talk about things like money and people's differences. I agree with her, but it's hard for me to say it. Especially because in some ways I know I'm just jealous.

"Now, Cathy, how are you coming with the reading-tutors project?" Mrs. Inman asked me.

"Well, see, I was waiting for you to help me get in touch with Allen School, and then I was away being suspended," I said. "So I haven't really got started yet." I wished I had. Why didn't I think about it last week?

"Come on, Cathy," she said, sort of disapprovingly, "you don't need me to put you in touch with Allen School, do you really? What's the name of the teacher there your mother worked with?"

"Mrs. Pflaum."

"The way to begin is just to call Mrs. Pflaum and ask her."

I was surprised. I hadn't expected to do the arranging myself. I thought that Mrs. Inman would call them first and explain the project. The thing is, I am sort of embarrassed about making phone calls. ■

✔ Enter your reading time below. Then look up your reading speed on the Words-per-Minute table on page 130.

    Reading Time   _____

    Reading Speed   _____

Enter your reading speed on the Reading Speed graph on page 131.

Comprehension

Put an **X** in the box next to the correct answer for each question or statement. Do not look back at the selection.

1. Mrs. Inman is
   - ☐ a. the principal at Camden High.
   - ☐ b. a teacher at Camden High.
   - ☐ c. Karen's mother.

2. How did Mrs. Inman learn that the girls had been suspended?
   - ☐ a. She received a letter from school.
   - ☐ b. She read it in the teachers' announcements.
   - ☐ c. She read it in the newspaper.

3. Karen and Cathy were suspended for
   - ☐ a. cutting gym class.
   - ☐ b. visiting a boarding school.
   - ☐ c. going to The Break.

4. During the suspension, Cathy
   - ☐ a. cleaned house and painted.
   - ☐ b. worked at the Allen School.
   - ☐ c. interviewed at a boarding school.

5. The boarding school was located in
   - ☐ a. Camden.
   - ☐ b. New York.
   - ☐ c. Connecticut.

6. How did Mrs. Inman react when Karen told her she was going away to boarding school?
   - ☐ a. She was proud of Karen.
   - ☐ b. She was sorry Karen was leaving.
   - ☐ c. She was happy Karen was leaving.

7. Why did Cathy think Mrs. Inman was so frank?
   - ☐ a. She didn't think the girls' suspensions were so terrible.
   - ☐ b. She would just come out and talk about things like money and people's differences.
   - ☐ c. She told Cathy to call Mrs. Pflaum.

8. Cathy was supposed to help at the Allen School by being a
   - ☐ a. reading tutor.
   - ☐ b. hallway monitor.
   - ☐ c. cafeteria assistant.

✎ _____ Number of correct answers
Enter this number on the Comprehension graph on page 132.

Critical Thinking

Put an **X** in the box next to the best answer for each question or statement. You may look back at the selection if you'd like.

1. The author tells this story mainly by
   - ☐ a. comparing public high schools with boarding schools.
   - ☐ b. using her imagination and creativity.
   - ☐ c. retelling personal experiences.

2. Who is the narrator of this story?
   - ☐ a. Cathy
   - ☐ b. Karen
   - ☐ c. Julia

3. Why is Karen going to boarding school?
   - ☐ a. Her mother thinks she'll get a better education there.
   - ☐ b. She was suspended from Camden High.
   - ☐ c. She didn't like it at Camden High.

4. Which event happened first?
   - ☐ a. Karen and Cathy went to The Break after their gym class was cancelled.
   - ☐ b. Karen went for an interview at a boarding school.
   - ☐ c. Karen and Cathy were suspended from school.

5. The boarding school Karen talks about has only 60 students because
   - ☐ a. few students want to go there.
   - ☐ b. the classes are very difficult.
   - ☐ c. the number of students who can enter is limited.

6. Which of the following is a statement of opinion rather than fact?
   - ☐ a. "I went with Mom on Friday to talk to people from this one school in Connecticut."
   - ☐ b. "I always think one of the good things about Camden is the mixture of people who go to it."
   - ☐ c. "Hello, girls. I see in the teachers' announcements that you were suspended last week."

7. Which word best describes Mrs. Inman's attitude?
   - ☐ a. concerned
   - ☐ b. angry
   - ☐ c. threatened

8. Mrs. Inman won't arrange things for Cathy because she
   - ☐ a. doesn't know what Cathy wants.
   - ☐ b. isn't sure how to arrange things.
   - ☐ c. wants Cathy to do it herself.

✎ _____ Number of correct answers
Enter this number on the Critical Thinking graph on page 133.

Vocabulary

Each numbered sentence contains an underlined word from the selection. Following are three definitions. Put an **X** in the box next to the best meaning of the word as it is used in the sentence.

1. "Please excuse Cathy for being absent. She was <u>suspended</u>."
   - ☐ a. not allowed to attend
   - ☐ b. traveling
   - ☐ c. very sick

2. I hadn't <u>expected</u> Karen to decide so fast. I was surprised.
   - ☐ a. been prepared for
   - ☐ b. wanted
   - ☐ c. seen

3. "But I'm <u>definitely</u> going to go to boarding school somewhere."
   - ☐ a. possibly
   - ☐ b. recently
   - ☐ c. surely

4. "I went for an <u>interview</u> at a boarding school."
   - ☐ a. dinner
   - ☐ b. class
   - ☐ c. meeting

5. "I always think one of the good things about Camden is the <u>mixture</u> of people who go to it."
   - ☐ a. total
   - ☐ b. blend
   - ☐ c. nature

6. I don't know anyone else who would just come out and talk about things like money and people's <u>differences</u>.
   - ☐ a. contrasts
   - ☐ b. problems
   - ☐ c. similarities

7. "Come on, Cathy," she said, sort of <u>disapprovingly</u>.
   - ☐ a. with great anger
   - ☐ b. not being pleased
   - ☐ c. hopelessly

8. The thing is, I am sort of <u>embarrassed</u> about making phone calls.
   - ☐ a. excited
   - ☐ b. terrified
   - ☐ c. shy

✎ _____ Number of correct answers
Enter this number on the Vocabulary graph on page 134.

Personal Response

Describe a time when a friend moved or went to a different school.

_____

_____

✔ Check Your Progress
Study the graphs you completed for Lessons 1–10 and answer the How Am I Doing? questions on page 135.

11 | Bats Incredible!

by Arlene Schnippert

Many people are afraid of bats. Are you one of them? There really is no good reason to fear them. As you'll learn in this selection, bats really are quite incredible!

Bats! Hundreds of thousands of bats spiraled upward out of the dark mouth of the cave like a black cloud of living flesh. What would your reactions be to such a sight? Fear? Revulsion? Thoughts of vampires and dank caves?

The bat would probably never make the "pet of the month" club. However, when you look into the life and habits of bats, you will soon see that this creature is indeed amazing and incredible!

Our whole family became interested in the subject of bats when my middle daughter was assigned a research report and chose bats as her subject. Soon we were all "oohing" and "aahing" over pictures of bats. To our surprise, we found the bat to be a complex, interesting animal.

Then, on a trip last summer through New Mexico, we stopped at Carlsbad Caverns. We spent the day touring this natural wonder, and then came back at dusk to watch the bats in flight. Nearly 300,000 bats leave the cave at sundown to feed throughout the night and then return near dawn to their cave roost. It was a sight to see these Mexican freetail bats come swarming out of the cave, at a rate of about 5,000 bats a minute, for nearly an hour.

Bats are the only mammals that can fly, and they make up the second largest group of mammals in the animal world. There are more than 900 species of bats. They only come out at night to feed. During the day they hang upside down in sheltered places such as caves and trees. Most bats live in colonies that may have as many as several million members.

The size of a bat can be from a few inches to several feet in length. The largest bats have a wingspread of more than five feet, and a body the size of a pigeon. Some bats can fly as fast as 15 miles an hour, but most travel at only about half that speed.

Even though some bats depend on their vision and sense of smell to navigate at night, most use a phenomenon called echolocation. The bats make a series of short, high-pitched sounds as they fly. These sounds are reflected back to them from prey or other objects as echoes. From the echoes, the bats can figure out the direction and distance of objects in the area.

Most of these sounds bats make are too high-pitched for humans to hear. As the bats came out of the Carlsbad Caverns, we heard nothing but the soft swish of their wings.

Most people have heard of vampire bats and get the idea that bats in general will attack humans and feed on their blood! Only a few of the hundreds of types of bats live on blood. The bat that is called the vampire bat is found in parts of Central and South America, and it feeds mainly on small animals. Only rarely will it bite a human. And it doesn't suck all the blood from an animal, but only takes about one tablespoon.

Most species of bats feed either on insects, fish, small rodents, plants, or fruit. Actually they do little harm and instead they benefit humans by eating large numbers of destructive insects. They may eat as much as half their weight in food each night! Bats often rest during their night flights, digesting one meal, and then eating more.

Unlike many mammals, a bat's body temperature, breathing rate, and heartbeat vary greatly. They depend on the bat's activities and the temperature. Many bats hibernate or migrate during winter because of low temperatures and poor food supplies. They spend each winter in the same cave and each summer in the same roost.

Many times, the males and females occupy totally different roosts. Then for a few weeks each year, they come together for the mating season.

Most female bats have only one or two babies a year. These newborns from the start must cling to their mothers or to the roost because bats do not build nests. A baby bat may cling to its mother for perhaps its first week, even while she is flying and feeding at night.

Even though you may not want to cuddle up to a bat or have one roosting in your closet, you can still appreciate some of its amazing qualities.

If you see some bats flying at dusk one evening, instead of feeling fear or disgust, you may think to yourself, Bats really ARE incredible! ∎

✔ Enter your reading time below. Then look up your reading speed on the Words-per-Minute table on page 130.

   Reading Time   _____

   Reading Speed   _____

Enter your reading speed on the Reading Speed graph on page 131.

Comprehension

Put an **X** in the box next to the correct answer for each question or statement. Do not look back at the selection.

1. The bats leave Carlsbad Caverns at
   - ☐ a. midnight.
   - ☐ b. dusk.
   - ☐ c. closing time.

2. What kind of bats live in the Carlsbad Caverns?
   - ☐ a. Mexican freetail bats
   - ☐ b. vampire bats
   - ☐ c. miniature bats

3. Bats are the only mammals that can
   - ☐ a. fly.
   - ☐ b. swim.
   - ☐ c. climb.

4. How large can bat colonies get?
   - ☐ a. several hundred bats
   - ☐ b. several thousand bats
   - ☐ c. several million bats

5. Vampire bats feed mainly on
   - ☐ a. small animals.
   - ☐ b. insects.
   - ☐ c. humans.

6. Bats benefit human beings by
   - ☐ a. eating insects.
   - ☐ b. flying only at night.
   - ☐ c. providing a source of food.

7. A bat's body temperature, breathing rate, and heartbeat
   - ☐ a. depend on its size.
   - ☐ b. depend on its activities.
   - ☐ c. are determined by its diet.

50

8. How many babies do most female bats have each year?
   ☐ a. five
   ☐ b. three
   ☐ c. two

_____ Number of correct answers
Enter this number on the Comprehension graph on page 132.

Critical Thinking

Put an **X** in the box next to the best answer for each question or statement. You may look back at the selection if you'd like.

1. The author probably wrote this selection in order to
   ☐ a. inform you about the habits and qualities of bats.
   ☐ b. persuade you that bats can be dangerous.
   ☐ c. entertain you with scary bat stories.

2. How can bats hear sounds we can't?
   ☐ a. They hear at higher frequencies than we do.
   ☐ b. They make high-pitched sounds.
   ☐ c. They use echolocation.

3. Most bats use echolocation instead of their vision because
   ☐ a. they are often blind.
   ☐ b. they fly in swarms.
   ☐ c. it is more useful in the dark.

4. Choose the word the author uses to describe bats.
   ☐ a. vicious
   ☐ b. interesting
   ☐ c. frightening

5. Many people believe bats will attack humans and feed on their blood because they
   ☐ a. have read stories about bats attacking humans.
   ☐ b. have seen bats attack people on TV and in the movies.
   ☐ c. have heard of vampire bats and think all bats are like them.

6. Which of the following is a statement of opinion rather than fact?
   ☐ a. The bat would probably never make the "pet of the month" club.
   ☐ b. The size of the bat can be from a few inches to several feet in length.
   ☐ c. The bat that is called the vampire bat is found in parts of Central and South America.

7. Which of the following statements best expresses the main idea of the selection?
   ☐ a. Bats are amazing mammals that do little harm and benefit people.
   ☐ b. Bats make up the second largest group of mammals in the world.
   ☐ c. Many people have feelings of fear and revulsion when they see bats.

8. Which of the following does not fit with the other two?
   ☐ a. Carlsbad Caverns
   ☐ b. Central America
   ☐ c. New Mexico

_____ Number of correct answers
Enter this number on the Critical Thinking graph on page 133.

Vocabulary

Each numbered sentence contains an underlined word from the selection. Following are three definitions. Put an X in the box next to the best meaning of the word as it is used in the sentence.

1. What would your reactions be to such a sight? Fear? Revulsion?
   - ☐ a. anger
   - ☐ b. joy
   - ☐ c. disgust

2. You will soon see that this creature is indeed amazing and incredible!
   - ☐ a. not describable
   - ☐ b. frightening
   - ☐ c. hard to believe

3. During the day they hang upside down in sheltered places such as caves and trees.
   - ☐ a. protected
   - ☐ b. scattered
   - ☐ c. shaded

4. Even though some bats depend on their vision and sense of smell to navigate at night, most use a phenomenon called echolocation.
   - ☐ a. fly
   - ☐ b. find direction
   - ☐ c. communicate

5. Only rarely will it bite a human.
   - ☐ a. not very often
   - ☐ b. in anger
   - ☐ c. in fear

6. They spend each winter in the same cave and each summer in the same roost.
   - ☐ a. area
   - ☐ b. resting place
   - ☐ c. tree

7. Many times, the males and females occupy totally different roosts.
   - ☐ a. return to
   - ☐ b. live in
   - ☐ c. abandon

8. You can still appreciate some of its amazing qualities.
   - ☐ a. deny
   - ☐ b. obscure
   - ☐ c. enjoy

_____ **Number of correct answers**
Enter this number on the Vocabulary graph on page 134.

Personal Response

What was the most surprising or interesting thing you learned about bats in this selection?

_____

_____

What would you say to someone who says that bats are terrible, disgusting creatures?

_____

_____

12 | The Twenty-One Balloons

by William Pène du Bois

This passage tells about the curious adventures of an American professor marooned on a small, supposedly uninhabited island.

After having slept for what must have been four or five hours, I found myself being gently awakened. I opened my eyes. My body was bright red from sun and sandburn. I looked up at what I thought was a man kneeling over me, shaking my shoulder and saying in perfect English, "Wake up, man, you've got to get some things on and get out of the sun, wake up." I thought that this must be part of some delirious dream. The idea of a man who spoke English on a small volcanic island in the Pacific seemed so odd. I shut my eyes again. But as soon as I did this, I felt my shoulder again being shaken and heard this same voice which kept saying, "Wake up, you've got to get in the shade!"

I shook my head and opened my eyes again. There was a man kneeling over me. As I sat up he stood up. He was handing me some clothes, and he was dressed in a most unusual manner. This man wasn't a native, and didn't suggest an explorer or a traveler. He looked like an overdressed aristocrat, lost on this seemingly desolate volcanic island. He was wearing a correctly tailored white morning suit—if you can imagine such a suit—with pin-stripe pants, white ascot tie, and a white cork bowler. The suit he was urging me to put on was just the same as the one he had on, only in my size.

"Am I dead?" I asked. "Is this Heaven?"

"No, my good man," he answered. "This isn't Heaven. This is the Pacific Island of Krakatoa."

Only recently there had been news stories telling that half of Krakatoa had blown up in the greatest volcanic eruption of all times.

"But I always thought Krakatoa was uninhabited," I told the gentleman in the white morning suit as I started painfully to put on the clothes he was handing me. "I always heard that the volcanic mountain made living on the Island impossible."

"This is Krakatoa, all right," he said. "And we who live here are most pleased that the rest of the world is still convinced that Krakatoa is uninhabited. Hurry up, put on your clothes."

I had put on the white pin-stripe trousers and the shirt as the gentleman handed them to me. The shirt had starched cuffs, a small white starched dickey, and a detachable wing collar. I didn't bother putting on the collar, and started rolling up my sleeves. "Let's go, lead on," I said.

"Come, come," said the gentleman from Krakatoa. "You can't come and visit us like that. Is that the way you would call on respectable people in San Francisco, New York, London, or Paris? Roll down those sleeves. Put on this collar, vest, and coat." As he was saying this he was smiling warmly to show that he meant no ill feeling but was merely setting me straight on Krakatoa style and manners. "I'll admit," he continued, "that on other islands in the Pacific it is considered quite the thing to give up shaving, forego haircuts, and wear whatever battered white ducks and soft shirts are available. Here, we prefer a more elegant mode of life. You, sir," he said, "are our first visitor. I am quite certain that you will be rather impressed with the way we live and with the various aspects of our Island. I hope you will be impressed anyhow, for since we believe in keeping this place absolutely secret, I believe you will be finding yourself spending the rest of your life as our guest."

While he was talking, I had obediently rolled down my sleeves. He handed me a pair of cuff links made simply of four diamonds the size of lima beans. He handed me diamond studs with which to do up my shirt front. I attached my wing collar. He held a small mirror so that I might more easily tie my white ascot. As I donned my white bowler, I was filled with many emotions. I thought that this was without doubt the most extravagantly absurd situation in which I had ever found myself. I was also giving a large amount of thought to that remark of his about being a guest of the people of Krakatoa for life. It was with deep, mixed feelings that I assured the gentleman that I was already quite impressed. ■

✔ Enter your reading time below. Then look up your reading speed on the Words-per-Minute table on page 130.

Reading Time   _____

Reading Speed   _____

Enter your reading speed on the Reading Speed graph on page 131.

Comprehension

Put an **X** in the box next to the correct answer for each question or statement. Do not look back at the selection.

1. The man who wakes the narrator speaks
   - ☐ a. Krakatoan.
   - ☐ b. English.
   - ☐ c. Japanese.

2. The man is wearing
   - ☐ a. a native costume.
   - ☐ b. white ducks and a soft shirt.
   - ☐ c. a white morning suit.

3. The island the narrator finds himself on is located in the
   - ☐ a. Atlantic Ocean.
   - ☐ b. Indian Ocean.
   - ☐ c. Pacific Ocean.

4. What had the narrator learned about Krakatoa from recent news stories?
   - ☐ a. Half of the island had been blown up in a great volcanic eruption.
   - ☐ b. Krakatoa was a place that had an elegant mode of life.
   - ☐ c. Krakatoa was a place that was uninhabitable.

5. The man was concerned about the narrator's
   - ☐ a. rudeness.
   - ☐ b. clothes.
   - ☐ c. appetite.

6. The man wants to be sure that the information that there are people on the island is
   - ☐ a. reported in news stories.
   - ☐ b. known only by the narrator's friends.
   - ☐ c. kept a secret.

7. The cuff links the man gives to the narrator are made of
   - ☐ a. lima beans.
   - ☐ b. pearls.
   - ☐ c. diamonds.

8. What was the narrator giving quite a lot of thought to?
   - ☐ a. who the man was
   - ☐ b. whether he was dressed properly
   - ☐ c. the man's remarks about being a guest on Krakatoa for life

---

✎ _____ Number of correct answers
Enter this number on the Comprehension graph on page 132.

Critical Thinking

Put an ✘ in the box next to the best answer for each question or statement. You may look back at the selection if you'd like.

1. Which choice best describes this story?
   - ☐ a. a story made up by the author using his imagination and creativity
   - ☐ b. a story of a real person's life written by that person
   - ☐ c. a story of a real person's life written by someone else

2. The people of Krakatoa are very concerned about their
   - ☐ a. wildlife.
   - ☐ b. diet.
   - ☐ c. appearance.

3. Which word best describes the narrator's condition when he wakes up?
   - ☐ a. sick
   - ☐ b. confused
   - ☐ c. excited

4. Based on what you've read, you can predict that the narrator will probably
   - ☐ a. choose to stay on the island.
   - ☐ b. be prevented from leaving the island.
   - ☐ c. leave the island on the next ship.

5. The rest of the world is convinced that Krakatoa is uninhabited because
   - ☐ a. that part of the ocean is too hot.
   - ☐ b. there is no food and little water there.
   - ☐ c. there is a volcanic mountain on the island.

6. Which of the following is a statement of opinion rather than fact?
   - ☐ a. This man wasn't a native, and didn't suggest an explorer or traveler.
   - ☐ b. "This isn't Heaven. This is the Pacific Island of Krakatoa."
   - ☐ c. "I am quite certain you will be rather impressed with the way we live and the various aspects of our Island."

7. In which way is life on Krakatoa different from life on the other Pacific islands?
   - ☐ a. Life is more elegant on Krakatoa.
   - ☐ b. Life is more casual on Krakatoa.
   - ☐ c. People live longer on Krakatoa.

8. Choose the sentence that correctly restates the following sentence from the selection: "And we who live here are most pleased that the rest of the world is still convinced that Krakatoa is uninhabited."
   - ☐ a. We are happy that everyone believes no one lives on Krakatoa.
   - ☐ b. Those who live on Krakatoa like to pretend they live alone.
   - ☐ c. We like Krakatoa because it is different from other places.

✎ _____ Number of correct answers
Enter this number on the Critical Thinking graph on page 133.

Vocabulary

Each numbered sentence contains an underlined word from the selection. Following are three definitions. Put an **X** in the box next to the best meaning of the word as it is used in the sentence.

1. I thought that this must be part of some <u>delirious</u> dream.
   - [ ] a. pleasant
   - [ ] b. crazy
   - [ ] c. forgotten

2. He looked like an overdressed aristocrat, lost on this seemingly <u>desolate</u> volcanic island.
   - [ ] a. popular
   - [ ] b. crowded
   - [ ] c. deserted

3. The suit he was <u>urging</u> me to put on was just the same as the one he had on, only in my size.
   - [ ] a. allowing
   - [ ] b. pushing
   - [ ] c. removing

4. Half of Krakatoa had blown up in the greatest volcanic <u>eruption</u> of all times.
   - [ ] a. song
   - [ ] b. explosion
   - [ ] c. shout

5. "And we who live here are most pleased that the rest of the world is still convinced that Krakatoa is <u>uninhabited</u>."
   - [ ] a. informal
   - [ ] b. cold
   - [ ] c. without people

6. "Is that the way you would call on <u>respectable</u> people in San Francisco, New York, London, or Paris?"
   - [ ] a. proper
   - [ ] b. lonely
   - [ ] c. elderly

7. "It is considered quite the thing to give up shaving, <u>forego</u> haircuts, and wear whatever battered white ducks and soft shirts are available."
   - [ ] a. give up
   - [ ] b. overdo
   - [ ] c. change

8. "Here, we prefer a more elegant <u>mode</u> of life."
   - [ ] a. movement
   - [ ] b. way
   - [ ] c. result

✎ _____ Number of correct answers
Enter this number on the Vocabulary graph on page 134.

Personal Response

Why do you think the people on the island of Krakatoa want their existence kept a secret?

_____

_____

What will become of the narrator? Write two or three sentences to describe his fate.

_____

_____

_____

13 | Exploring the Last Frontier

Scientists know little about the bottom of the sea. But would the expense and risks of exploring the ocean depths be worth it?

Humans have climbed Mount Everest. They have crossed the Sahara Desert and even lived at the South Pole. But one place on Earth that remains unconquered is the floor of the ocean. Scientists know more about the moon and Mars than they do about the bottom of the sea. The ocean abyss is truly Earth's last great frontier.

Just how deep is the ocean? On average, it is about 2.3 miles deep. But some places are much deeper than that. The Mariana Trench lies under the Pacific Ocean. It is a 1,584-mile-long crevasse, or deep crack, in the ocean floor. The deepest part of the trench is called Challenger Deep. At more than 36,000 feet down, it is the deepest spot in the world. That's a depth of nearly seven miles—a mile and a half deeper than Mount Everest is high.

People once thought that the ocean floor was flat and dull. Now they know better: the bottom of the ocean is much rougher than dry land. It has huge canyons, some of which are deep enough and large enough to hide the Rocky Mountains. The ocean floor also has its own mountain ranges. They are massive; one such range is more than 31,000 miles long. Circling the globe, it makes its way through all four of the world's oceans.

The ocean has kept its secrets well. In some ways, it is harder to explore the seas than to explore outer space. One reason is that a human being, without help, can dive down only about 10 feet. Beyond that depth, pressure starts to build on the lungs and inner ear. In any case, even the best diver can't hold his or her breath longer than two or three minutes.

Today, of course, divers can go much deeper than ever before. Those who use scuba gear can go down more than 100 feet. Scuba divers rarely go below 150 feet, though, for there is too much pressure. Coming back up can also be a problem. The change in pressure can cause the bends. A bad case can be fatal. Wearing a pressurized suit, however, a diver can go down about 1,400 feet. From that point to the deepest part of the ocean is still a long distance.

In 1960, Donald Walsh and Jacques Piccard climbed into a small metal sphere. It was a bathyscaphe—a watertight cabin used for deep-sea diving. Named the *Trieste*, the cabin carried nothing but the two men. It had no cameras to take pictures or arms to collect objects. The question was simple: could the two men go to the bottom of the Mariana Trench and come back alive?

It took Walsh and Piccard an hour and a half to descend 10,000 feet. Two hours later, they had gone down 32,000 feet. Pressure at this depth was immense—almost 14,000 pounds per square inch. After another hour, Walsh and Piccard were just 250 feet from the bottom of the ocean. Very slowly, they dropped down to the ocean floor. They had made it.

That event happened a long time ago. Science has made great progress since then. Yet no one has ever duplicated Walsh's and Piccard's feat. No one has even come close. The reason is money—the trips are too costly.

In addition, some people aren't sure that exploring the ocean is worth the effort. Robert Ballard is the scientist who found the wreck of the *Titanic*. "I believe that the deep sea has very little to offer," he says. "I don't see the future there."

Jean Jarry, a top French ocean scientist, agrees. He doesn't feel that people should go below 20,000 feet. Only about 3 percent of the ocean is deeper than that. "To go beyond [20,000 feet] is not very interesting and is very expensive," Jarry says.

Others, however, disagree. Greg Stone, of the New England Aquarium, wants to go all the way down. He says, "We won't know what the ocean floor holds until we've been there."

The Japanese also want to explore the ocean abyss. In 1995, they sent an unmanned probe named *Kaiko* to the bottom of Challenger Deep. *Kaiko* sent back pictures of things that were hard to believe—animals able to live at that depth. When they were there, Walsh and Piccard said they had seen a fish, but at the time few people believed them. Most people felt that nothing could live at such a depth. But now there is information that such life is possible. ■

✔ **Enter your reading time below. Then look up your reading speed on the Words-per-Minute table on page 130.**

Reading Time _____

Reading Speed _____

Enter your reading speed on the Reading Speed graph on page 131.

Comprehension

Put an ✘ in the box next to the correct answer for each question or statement. Do not look back at the selection.

1. The average depth of the ocean is about
   ☐ a. two miles.
   ☐ b. five miles.
   ☐ c. seven miles.

2. The deepest part of the sea lies under the
   ☐ a. Arctic Ocean.
   ☐ b. Atlantic Ocean.
   ☐ c. Pacific Ocean.

3. How deep is the deepest part of the ocean?
   ☐ a. less than 10,000 feet
   ☐ b. about 32,000 feet
   ☐ c. more than 36,000 feet

4. Wearing pressurized suits, divers are able to go down about
   ☐ a. 150 feet.
   ☐ b. 1,400 feet.
   ☐ c. 10,000 feet.

5. Who were the first humans to reach the bottom of the sea in a planned dive?
   ☐ a. Robert Ballard and Jean Jarry
   ☐ b. Donald Walsh and Jacques Piccard
   ☐ c. two Japanese scientists

6. No one has duplicated that dive to the deepest part of the ocean floor because
   ☐ a. it would be too dangerous.
   ☐ b. scientists are no longer interested in the bottom of the sea.
   ☐ c. it would be too costly.

7. One top ocean scientist feels that people should not go below 20,000 feet because
   - ☐ a. only about 3 percent of the ocean is deeper than that.
   - ☐ b. to go beyond that is not very interesting and is very expensive.
   - ☐ c. the sea pressure is too great beyond that depth.

8. Information gathered from probes to the deepest part of the ocean has proven that
   - ☐ a. life is possible at that depth.
   - ☐ b. nothing can live at that depth.
   - ☐ c. only seaweed can live at that depth.

✎ _____ **Number of correct answers**
Enter this number on the Comprehension graph on page 132.

Critical Thinking

Put an **X** in the box next to the best answer for each question or statement. You may look back at the selection if you'd like.

1. The author uses the first paragraph to
   - ☐ a. inform you of some of the great accomplishments of humans.
   - ☐ b. compare scientists' knowledge of Earth and space with their knowledge of the bottom of the sea.
   - ☐ c. describe the floor of the ocean.

2. Which of the following best expresses the main idea of the selection?
   - ☐ a. Scientists know more about the moon and Mars than they do about the bottom of the sea.
   - ☐ b. It is risky and expensive to explore the bottom of the sea.
   - ☐ c. Scientists know little about the bottom of the sea, and disagree about whether to learn more.

3. You can conclude that the main reason scientists have so little knowledge about the bottom of the sea is that
   - ☐ a. it would take too much time to explore.
   - ☐ b. it's too expensive to explore.
   - ☐ c. scientists have no interest in exploring it.

4. Which event happened last?
   - ☐ a. Robert Ballard found the wreck of the *Titanic*.
   - ☐ b. Donald Walsh and Jacques Piccard went to the bottom of the Mariana Trench in the *Trieste*.
   - ☐ c. The Japanese sent an unmanned probe named *Kaiko* to the bottom of Challenger Deep.

5. One reason it's harder to explore the seas than to explore outer space is that
   - ☐ a. it's much more expensive.
   - ☐ b. it's harder to move through sea water than it is through space.
   - ☐ c. humans cannot withstand sea pressure below 10 feet without using some sort of protective equipment.

6. Which of the following is a statement of opinion rather than fact?
   - ☐ a. Scientists know more about the moon and Mars than they do about the bottom of the sea.
   - ☐ b. "I believe the deep sea has very little to offer."
   - ☐ c. At more than 36,000 feet down, Challenger Deep is the deepest spot in the world.

7. Compared to Mount Everest, the average depth of the ocean is
☐ a. deeper than Everest is high.
☐ b. less deep than Everest is high.
☐ c. about as deep as Everest is high.

8. Which of the following does *not* fit with the other two?
☐ a. the *Titanic*
☐ b. the *Trieste*
☐ c. the *Kaiko*

✎ _____ Number of correct answers
Enter this number on the Critical Thinking graph on page 133.

Vocabulary

Each numbered sentence contains an underlined word from the selection. Following are three definitions. Put an **X** in the box next to the best meaning of the word as it is used in the sentence.

1. They are <u>massive</u>; one such range is more than 31,000 miles long.
☐ a. very tall
☐ b. very large
☐ c. very rough

2. Those who use scuba <u>gear</u> can go down more than 100 feet.
☐ a. fins
☐ b. boats
☐ c. equipment

3. A bad case can be <u>fatal</u>.
☐ a. uncomfortable
☐ b. deadly
☐ c. serious

4. It took Walsh and Piccard an hour and a half to <u>descend</u> 10,000 feet.
☐ a. go up
☐ b. go down
☐ c. travel

5. Pressure at this depth was <u>immense</u>— almost 14,000 pounds per square inch.
☐ a. very great
☐ b. not large
☐ c. noticeable

6. Science has made great <u>progress</u>.
☐ a. experiments
☐ b. improvements
☐ c. pioneers

7. Yet no one has ever <u>duplicated</u> Walsh's and Piccard's feat.
☐ a. denied
☐ b. attempted
☐ c. repeated

8. The Japanese also want to explore the ocean <u>abyss</u>.
☐ a. place of great depth
☐ b. place at a highest point
☐ c. place under the surface

✎ _____ Number of correct answers
Enter this number on the Vocabulary graph on page 134.

Personal Response

The scientist Robert Ballard has said, "I believe that the deep sea has very little to offer." Do you agree or disagree? Explain your answer.

_____

_____

14 | To Build a Fire

by Jack London

In this passage from the short story a man sets out alone in the bitter cold of the Yukon Territory to meet his friends at a distant camp.

Day had broken exceedingly cold and gray, when the man turned aside from the main Yukon trail and climbed the high earthbank, where a dim and little-traveled trail led eastward through the fat spruce timberland. It was a steep bank, and he paused for breath at the top, excusing the act to himself by looking at his watch. It was nine o'clock. There was no sun nor hint of sun, though there was not a cloud in the sky. It was a clear day, and yet there seemed an intangible pall over the face of things, a subtle gloom that made the day dark, and that was due to the absence of sun. This fact did not worry the man. He was used to the lack of sun. It had been days since he had seen the sun, and he knew that a few more days must pass before that cheerful orb, due south, would just peep above the skyline and dip immediately from view.

The man flung a look back along the way he had come. The Yukon lay a mile wide and hidden under three feet of ice. On top of this ice were as many feet of snow. It was all pure white, rolling in gentle undulations where the ice-jams of the freeze-up had formed. North and south, as far as his eye could see, it was unbroken white, save for a dark hairline that was the trail that led south five hundred miles to the Chilcoot Pass.

But all this—the mysterious, far-reaching hairline trail, the absence of sun from the sky, the tremendous cold, and the strangeness and weirdness of it all—made no impression on the man. He was a newcomer in the land and this was his first winter. The trouble with him was that he was without imagination. He was quick and alert in the things of life, but only in the things, and not in the significances. Fifty degrees below zero meant eighty-odd degrees of frost. Such fact impressed him as being cold and uncomfortable, and that was all. It did not lead him to meditate upon his frailty in general, able only to live within certain narrow limits of heat and cold; and from there on it did not lead him to the conjectural field of immortality and man's place in the universe. Fifty degrees below zero stood for a bit of frost that hurt and that must be guarded against by the use of mittens, earflaps, warm moccasins, and thick socks. Fifty degrees below zero was to him just precisely fifty degrees below zero. That there should be anything more to it than that was a thought that never entered his head.

As he turned to go on, he spat speculatively. There was a sharp, explosive crackle that startled him. He spat again. And again, in the air, before it could fall to the snow, the spittle crackled. He knew that at fifty below spittle crackled on the snow, but this spittle had crackled in the air. Undoubtedly it was colder than fifty below— how much colder he did not know. But the temperature did not matter. He was bound for the old claim on the left fork of Henderson Creek where the boys were already. They had come over across the divide from the Indian Creek country, while he had come the roundabout way to take a look at the possibilities of getting out logs in the spring from the islands in the Yukon. He would be in to camp by six o'clock; a bit after dark, it was true, but the boys would be there, a fire would be going, and a hot supper would be ready. As for lunch, he pressed his hand against the protruding bundle under his jacket. It was also under his shirt, wrapped up in a handkerchief and lying against the naked skin. It was the only way to keep the biscuits from freezing.

He plunged in among the big spruce trees. The trail was faint. He was glad he was without a sled, traveling light. In fact, he carried nothing but the lunch wrapped in the handkerchief. He was surprised, however, at the cold. It certainly was cold, he concluded, as he rubbed his numb nose and cheekbones with his mittened hand. ■

✔ **Enter your reading time below. Then look up your reading speed on the Words-per-Minute table on page 130.**

Reading Time _____

Reading Speed _____

Enter your reading speed on the Reading Speed graph on page 131.

Comprehension

Put an **✗** in the box next to the correct answer for each question or statement. Do not look back at the selection.

1. This story takes place
   - ☐ a. in Siberia.
   - ☐ b. in the Yukon Territory.
   - ☐ c. during an Arctic expedition.

2. In what season is the story set?
   - ☐ a. winter
   - ☐ b. fall
   - ☐ c. spring

3. The sky above the man was
   - ☐ a. clear and cloudless.
   - ☐ b. bright with sunlight.
   - ☐ c. dim and cloudy.

4. The ice on the Yukon River was
   - ☐ a. as smooth as glass.
   - ☐ b. melting quickly.
   - ☐ c. frozen three feet thick.

5. The man was a
   - ☐ a. frequent visitor to the land.
   - ☐ b. newcomer to the land.
   - ☐ c. native of the land.

6. What was the temperature?
   - ☐ a. almost 50 degrees below zero
   - ☐ b. more than 50 degrees below zero
   - ☐ c. just 50 degrees below zero

7. Why was the man out walking in the snow?
   - ☐ a. He was lost and looking for the trail.
   - ☐ b. He was seeking help for his friends.
   - ☐ c. He was looking for ways of getting out logs in the spring.

8. The man expected to reach the camp
   - ☐ a. shortly after dark that day.
   - ☐ b. by mid-afternoon that day.
   - ☐ c. early the next morning.

✎ _____ **Number of correct answers**
Enter this number on the Comprehension graph on page 132.

Critical Thinking

Put an X in the box next to the best answer for each question or statement. You may look back at the selection if you'd like.

1. The main purpose of the first paragraph is to establish how
   - ☐ a. gloomy the day was.
   - ☐ b. lonely the man was.
   - ☐ c. cold the weather was.

2. What kind of mood or feeling does the author create in the story?
   - ☐ a. apprehensive
   - ☐ b. hopeless
   - ☐ c. cheerful

3. Why was the man glad he had no sled?
   - ☐ a. He didn't know how to use one.
   - ☐ b. He didn't need one for such a short trip.
   - ☐ c. He thought he could travel faster without one.

4. Based on what you've read, you can predict that the man will probably
   - ☐ a. reach camp without any trouble.
   - ☐ b. never each camp.
   - ☐ c. reach camp after experiencing a little trouble.

5. The bitter cold weather did not matter to the man because he
   - ☐ a. was dressed warmly.
   - ☐ b. thought he would be in camp in six hours.
   - ☐ c. found some shelter.

6. Which of these is a statement of opinion rather than fact?
   - ☐ a. There was no sun nor hint of sun, though there was not a cloud in the sky.
   - ☐ b. Fifty degrees below zero meant eighty-odd degrees of frost.
   - ☐ c. The trouble with him was that he was without imagination.

7. The man appears to be
   - ☐ a. lonely and frightened.
   - ☐ b. confused about direction.
   - ☐ c. calm and confident.

8. The word that best describes the man is
   - ☐ a. courageous
   - ☐ b. inexperienced
   - ☐ c. sensible

✎ _____ Number of correct answers
Enter this number on the Critical Thinking graph on page 133.

Vocabulary

Each numbered sentence contains an underlined word or phrase from the selection. Following are three definitions. Put an X in the box next to the best meaning of the word as it is used in the sentence.

1. It was a clear day, and yet there seemed an intangible pall over the face of things.
   - ☐ a. unseen
   - ☐ b. untouchable
   - ☐ c. inaudible

2. It was all pure white, rolling in gentle <u>undulations</u> where the ice-jams of the freeze-up had formed.
   - ☐ a. waves
   - ☐ b. balls
   - ☐ c. edges

3. North and south, as far as his eye could see, it was unbroken white, <u>save for</u> a dark hairline that was the trail.
   - ☐ a. in spite of
   - ☐ b. because of
   - ☐ c. except for

4. It did not lead him to meditate upon his <u>frailty</u> in general, able only to live within certain narrow limits of heat and cold.
   - ☐ a. strength
   - ☐ b. spirit
   - ☐ c. weakness

5. It did not lead him to the conjectural field of <u>immortality</u> and man's place in the universe.
   - ☐ a. eternal life
   - ☐ b. eternal problems
   - ☐ c. eternal fear

6. As he turned to go on, he spat <u>speculatively</u>.
   - ☐ a. with difficulty
   - ☐ b. thoughtfully
   - ☐ c. in surprise

7. They had come over across the divide from the Indian Creek country, while he had come the <u>roundabout</u> way.
   - ☐ a. longer
   - ☐ b. shorter
   - ☐ c. straighter

8. As for lunch, he pressed his hand against the <u>protruding</u> bundle under his jacket.
   - ☐ a. clumsy
   - ☐ b. sticking out
   - ☐ c. heavy

✎ _____ **Number of correct answers**
Enter this number on the Vocabulary graph on page 134.

Personal Response

Describe a personal experience when you were outside in either bitter cold or extremely hot weather.

_____

_____

_____

What advice would you have given the man before he set out alone to travel to the distant camp?

_____

_____

_____

15 | You Kids Are All Alike

This article makes you aware of what stereotyping is and the harm that it can cause.

Suppose you have to buy a present for each of the following people:

Harry Skinner, a cabdriver;
Freddy Faster, a seventh-grade A student;
Abigail Watson, a senior citizen.

Which of the following gifts would you choose for each:

a desk dictionary,
a rocking chair,
two tickets to the opera,
a pair of skis,
a leather jacket,
a theatrical makeup kit?

Did you choose

the leather jacket for Harry, because it's the kind of clothing a cabdriver wears?

the desk dictionary for Freddy, because he can always use a dictionary to help him with his studies?

the rocker for Abigail, because she probably doesn't get around too much anymore?

No doubt these are the usual choices. But the people on our list happen to be unusual.

Harry is a voice student who drives a cab in his spare time. He has nothing against leather jackets, but he would prefer the opera tickets. He hopes to become an opera singer someday.

Freddy is working on a clown routine for the school talent show right now. A theatrical makeup kit would help his act a lot more than a dictionary would.

Born in Vermont, Abigail still enjoys skiing. She would put those new skis to good use; she has no need of a rocking chair just yet.

Did the labels on these people mislead you into making the usual choices? Then you read too much into them. To know what a person is really like you need a great deal of information, more than you will find on a label. With nothing but a word or two to go by, your mind produced a "stereotyped" picture of the person rather than a real one.

In printing, a *stereotype* is a metal plate that reproduces the same picture over and over. The word *stereotype* is also used to mean a mental picture in which all people of a particular group look and act alike. When we think in stereotypes we cannot judge people fairly. Why? Because stereotypes ignore the fact that no two human beings are identical.

Take the cabdriver, for example. Did you picture him as a middle-aged, rugged, boisterous, gabby family man? That is one stereotype of a "cabbie"—the one you usually meet on TV or in the movies. But real cabdrivers can be young or old, sensitive, educated, soft-spoken, shy, unmarried, and either male or female. Yet, when we think in stereotypes, we tend to ignore the differences among people.

Some adults have a way of stereotyping young people. Perhaps you have heard their argument. It goes something like this:

"You kids are all alike. You show no respect for your elders, you have poor manners, and your speech is as sloppy as your dress. You don't realize how good you have it. Now in my day—"

The harm is that the person who believes in this stereotype may act on his or her belief. In the case just mentioned, you—as a young person—would be the victim. Maybe you have already had this type of experience. Have you ever met a merchant who doesn't trust kids in his store? a bus driver who hates all the kids who go to that school on the hill? a librarian who is suspicious of a boy with long hair?

Stereotypes are often used by mass media—by TV, advertising, movies, newspapers, and magazines. Sometimes these stereotypes are amusing and entertaining. The henpecked husband, the absentminded professor, the bearded hippie all make us laugh because they are such exaggerations of the real thing.

Stereotypes distort the truth by suggesting that all people in a particular group behave in the same way. They also suggest that only these people behave that way. Neither is true.

When people begin to stereotype others on the basis of race, religion, or nationality, the result is prejudice. It is important to remember that no one group in our society has a monopoly on brawls, laziness, crime, ignorance, foreign accents, drinking, greed, or pushiness. Nor does any one group have a monopoly on beauty, brains, glamour, strength, humor, or talent. Every group has its share of all these human qualities.

To be sure, a certain amount of stereotyping is bound to occur. We all do it, usually without thinking about it. But it's a good idea to remember that no two people in the world are identical. No label can be pasted on an individual or group that accurately describes that person or group. After all, labels belong on products, not on people. ■

✔ Enter your reading time below. Then look up your reading speed on the Words-per-Minute table on page 130.

Reading Time _____

Reading Speed _____

Enter your reading speed on the Reading Speed graph on page 131.

Comprehension

Put an **X** in the box next to the correct answer for each question or statement. Do not look back at the selection.

1. In this selection, who hopes to become an opera singer?
   - ☐ a. the senior citizen
   - ☐ b. the cabdriver
   - ☐ c. the seventh-grade student

2. Which person does the author say would enjoy the skis the most?
   - ☐ a. the cabdriver
   - ☐ b. the seventh-grade student
   - ☐ c. the senior citizen

3. The gift that would help Freddy the most is a
   - ☐ a. theatrical makeup kit.
   - ☐ b. desk dictionary.
   - ☐ c. leather jacket.

4. According to the selection, most people would assume that the leather jacket would most likely be worn by a
   - ☐ a. cabdriver.
   - ☐ b. seventh-grade student.
   - ☐ c. senior citizen.

5. What fact do stereotypes ignore?
   - ☐ a. Most human beings are alike.
   - ☐ b. Most people can be judged fairly.
   - ☐ c. No two human beings are identical.

6. How do stereotypes distort the truth?
   - ☐ a. by suggesting that all people in a group behave in the same way
   - ☐ b. by giving false information
   - ☐ c. by exaggerating the truth

7. An example given of a stereotype is the
   - ☐ a. funny comedian.
   - ☐ b. absentminded professor.
   - ☐ c. good teacher.

8. What results when people begin to stereotype others on the basis of race, religion, or nationality?
   - ☐ a. hurt feelings
   - ☐ b. prejudice
   - ☐ c. mutual understanding

✎ _____ Number of correct answers
Enter this number on the Comprehension graph on page 132.

Critical Thinking

Put an ✗ in the box next to the best answer for each question or statement. You may look back at the selection if you'd like.

1. The author wrote this selection to
   - ☐ a. make you laugh at certain groups.
   - ☐ b. show that some stereotypes are true.
   - ☐ c. convince you not to stereotype people.

2. Why does the author ask you to choose a present for three people?
   - ☐ a. to illustrate a point
   - ☐ b. to test your judgment
   - ☐ c. to see how generous you are

3. Which of the following statements best expresses the main idea of the selection?
   - ☐ a. People who believe in stereotypes may act on those beliefs.
   - ☐ b. People who think in stereotypes, cannot judge others fairly because they ignore the fact that no two people are identical.
   - ☐ c. Stereotypes used by the mass media are sometimes amusing and entertaining.

4. Which of the following statements is an example of stereotyping?
   - ☐ a. All American citizens have the right to vote.
   - ☐ b. All Italians like spaghetti.
   - ☐ c. All bats are mammals.

5. According to the selection, people sometimes stereotype individuals or groups because they
   - ☐ a. think it's funny.
   - ☐ b. want to.
   - ☐ c. lack enough information.

6. Which of the following is a statement of opinion rather than fact?
   - ☐ a. After all, labels belong on products, not on people.
   - ☐ b. In printing, a *stereotype* is a metal plate that reproduces the same picture over and over.
   - ☐ c. Stereotypes are often used by mass media.

7. The author says "labels belong on products, not on people." This means that
   - ☐ a. all labels are misleading.
   - ☐ b. unlabeled products are dangerous.
   - ☐ c. labels on people are misleading.

8. The word that best describes people who stereotype other individuals or groups is
   □ a. cruel.
   □ b. funny.
   □ c. uninformed.

✎ _____ Number of correct answers
Enter this number on the Critical Thinking graph on page 133.

Vocabulary

Each numbered sentence contains an underlined word from the selection. Following are three definitions. Put an **X** in the box next to the best meaning of the word as it is used in the sentence.

1. Did the labels on these people mislead you into making the usual choice?
   □ a. fool
   □ b. help
   □ c. force

2. The word *stereotype* is also used to mean a mental picture in which all people of a particular group look and act alike.
   □ a. certain
   □ b. random
   □ c. limited

3. Did you picture him as a middle-aged, rugged, boisterous, gabby family man?
   □ a. soft
   □ b. silent
   □ c. rowdy

4. "You don't realize how good you have it."
   □ a. show
   □ b. understand
   □ c. earn

5. Have you ever met a merchant who doesn't trust kids in his store?
   □ a. librarian
   □ b. police officer
   □ c. shop owner

6. The henpecked husband, the absentminded professor, the bearded hippie all make us laugh because they are such exaggerations of the real thing.
   □ a. opposites
   □ b. overstatements
   □ c. descriptions

7. Stereotypes distort the truth by suggesting that all people in a particular group behave the same way.
   □ a. reveal
   □ b. twist
   □ c. explain

8. But it's a good idea to remember that no two people in the world are identical.
   □ a. exactly alike
   □ b. agreeable
   □ c. particular

✎ _____ Number of correct answers
Enter this number on the Vocabulary graph on page 134.

Personal Response

State in your own words the most important thing you learned from this selection.

_____

_____

_____

16 | Snow Bound

by Harry Mazer

Snow Bound tells the story of two people struggling through a snowstorm. In this passage from the book, one of them, Tony, looks for his lost dog.

When Tony walked out on the bridge the cold caught him by surprise. The wind was sharper here, whistling under the abutments. "Here, boy," he yelled. "Here, Arthur." The wind whipped the words from his mouth. He went further, past the bridge to the stores at the end of Bridge Street. A fine, thin snow was falling, etching every crack and crevice. Danny Belco, on his way to school, hailed Tony. He waved Danny on. He wasn't going to school until he found his dog.

He crossed between the mattress shop and shoe store, over to Broadway, and back down past the Broadway Garage, where he could see his mother's blue 1951 Plymouth on the lot. He crossed the street and asked Frank Beach, the mechanic on duty, if he'd seen his dog. Frank was working the pumps outside, gassing up a green Dodge. "Nope," Frank shook his head. "Too cold to think about dogs."

Tony crisscrossed the neighborhood—Summit, Townsend, Bridge—stopping to ask anyone he met if they'd seen a medium-sized brown dog. Twice he checked the ravine, climbing down to the clubhouse, where the wind was really howling. He went home to warm up and use the bathroom; his aunt Irene's black Olds was in the driveway. She saw him before he could get away.

"What are you doing home? You're supposed to be in school." She peered at him suspiciously. Like her sister, his mother, she had four of her own, except hers were all boys, and she knew every trick in the book. "You're playing hookey, aren't you? Don't give me that innocent look, Anthony. You're not sweet-talking your mother now. This is me, Aunt Irene. You get to school, on-the-double. I'm going to call the principal's office in fifteen minutes, and you better be there. So move, big boy!" She got into her car, rolling down the window to say, "You go to school, Anthony, you hear me?"

"Yes," he said, following her as she backed out to the street, but the moment she was gone he went the opposite way. For the next hour he went over all the streets he'd covered already, without finding a trace of the dog. He was really cold now, stamping his feet and blowing on his fingers. Stubbornly he refused to give up the search. The longer it went on, the angrier he became. They hadn't even waked Tony to ask him if he knew some place for the dog. No, they'd simply kicked the dumb mutt out into the night because he made a little noise and woke up the landlords. As if Tony cared about the Bielics, always worrying about their house. When Mr. Bielic came upstairs to collect the rent on the first of the month, he would look at the floors and the walls. A little crack in the plaster and he had a fit. "Oh, ho, what's this, Mrs. Laporte!" He'd stretch his lips and shake his finger playfully, but he meant it. His precious house meant more to him than anything. More than a dog, for sure. And Tony's father had fallen right in with him. Tony's blood boiled every time he thought about it. His dog out in the snow, just because he'd made a little noise! What right did they have? It was *his* dog, nobody else's. Hot rage swept over him. Rage at his parents. It was the dog, but it was more than the dog. He didn't want to go home. He'd never go home. Once he let himself go, thinking this way, there was no bottom to the feeling of betrayal.

He went back to the gas station. Frank was in the garage. "Is it cold!" Frank said. "Find your dog yet?" Tony shook his head.

"Too bad." Frank blew his nose in a red handkerchief. "Anyone who works on a day like this has gotta be crazy. Right, kid?"

"Is my mother's car ready yet?" Tony asked. "I thought I'd warm it up if it was ready. Have you got the key?" He watched Frank take his mother's set of keys from the grease-stained key board behind the cash register.

"Put them back when you're done," Frank said.

Tony pocketed the keys and walked out to his mother's car. He was too young for a junior license, but ever since he'd been old enough to reach the pedals, he'd been driving cars around empty shopping centers and in the country around his Uncle Leonard's place. ∎

✔ Enter your reading time below. Then look up your reading speed on the Words-per-Minute table on page 130.

Reading Time   _____

Reading Speed   _____

Enter your reading speed on the Reading Speed graph on page 131.

Comprehension

Put an ✗ next to the correct answer for each question or statement. Do not look back at the selection.

1. Tony was looking for
   - ☐ a. his dog.
   - ☐ b. a job.
   - ☐ c. Danny Belco.

2. The first thing Tony noticed when he walked out on the bridge was
   - ☐ a. his mother.
   - ☐ b. Arthur.
   - ☐ c. the cold.

3. Who is the mechanic on duty in the Broadway Garage?
   - ☐ a. Danny Belco
   - ☐ b. Frank Beach
   - ☐ c. Tony's father

4. Aunt Irene wanted to
   - ☐ a. help Tony find his dog.
   - ☐ b. get her care repaired.
   - ☐ c. find out why Tony wasn't in school.

5. To be sure that Tony went to school, Aunt Irene was going to
   - ☐ a. call Tony's mother.
   - ☐ b. call the principal's office.
   - ☐ c. drive Tony to school.

6. Who was Mrs. Laporte?
   - ☐ a. the landlord's wife
   - ☐ b. another one of Tony's aunts
   - ☐ c. Tony's mother

7. Why had Tony's dog been kicked out into the night?
   - ☐ a. It made some noise and woke up Tony's parents.
   - ☐ b. It chewed up Tony's father's slippers.
   - ☐ c. It made some noise and woke up the landlords.

8. Tony was
- ☐ a. angry at his dog.
- ☐ b. angry at his family.
- ☐ c. kicked out of the house.

✎ _____ Number of correct answers
Enter this number on the Comprehension
graph on page 132.

Critical Thinking

Put an ✗ in the box next to the best answer
for each question or statement. You may look
back at the selection if you'd like.

1. The author intended this story to be
   - ☐ a. scary.
   - ☐ b. humorous.
   - ☐ c. serious.

2. Who is the narrator of this story?
   - ☐ a. an outside observer
   - ☐ b. Tony
   - ☐ c. Aunt Irene

3. This story takes place in the
   - ☐ a. winter.
   - ☐ b. spring.
   - ☐ c. fall.

4. Based on the way this passage ends, you
   can predict that Tony will probably
   - ☐ a. warm up his mother's car, and then
     put the keys back.
   - ☐ b. deliver the car back to his mother.
   - ☐ c. drive off in the car to get away from
     home.

5. Tony did not want to go home ever
   because he
   - ☐ a. couldn't keep his dog at home.
   - ☐ b. felt betrayed by his parents.
   - ☐ c. didn't like the landlord.

6. Which of the following is a statement of
   opinion rather than fact?
   - ☐ a. "I'm going to call the principal's
     office in 15 minutes."
   - ☐ b. "You're supposed to be in school."
   - ☐ c. "Anyone who works on a day like
     this has gotta be crazy."

7. Mr. Bielic worried about the floors and
   ceilings because he
   - ☐ a. was a professional carpenter.
   - ☐ b. did not want the landlord to see the
     cracks.
   - ☐ c. owned the house.

8. Choose the sentence that correctly
   restates the following sentence from the
   selection: "And Tony's father had fallen
   right in with him."
   - ☐ a. Tony's father was upset with him.
   - ☐ b. Tony's father felt the same way.
   - ☐ c. Tony's father and he fell down
     together.

✎ _____ Number of correct answers
Enter this number on the Critical Thinking
graph on page 133.

Vocabulary

Each numbered sentence contains an
underlined word from the selection.
Following are three definitions. Put an ✗ in
the box next to the best meaning of the word
as it is used in the sentence.

1. The wind was <u>sharper</u> here, whistling
   under the abutments.
   - ☐ a. warmer
   - ☐ b. quieter
   - ☐ c. colder

2. A fine, thin snow was falling, etching every crack and <u>crevice</u>.
   - ☐ a. slab
   - ☐ b. leaf
   - ☐ c. slit

3. Danny Belco, on his way to school, <u>hailed</u> Tony. He waved Danny on.
   - ☐ a. ignored
   - ☐ b. called to
   - ☐ c. tackled

4. Tony <u>crisscrossed</u> the neighborhood—Summit, Townsend, Bridge—stopping to ask anyone he met if they'd seen a medium-sized brown dog.
   - ☐ a. traveled back and forth
   - ☐ b. lost himself
   - ☐ c. avoided

5. She <u>peered</u> at him suspiciously.
   - ☐ a. asked suddenly
   - ☐ b. looked closely
   - ☐ c. smiled brightly

6. Mr. Bielic came upstairs to <u>collect</u> the rent on the first of the month.
   - ☐ a. pick up
   - ☐ b. return
   - ☐ c. steal

7. Hot <u>rage</u> swept over him.
   - ☐ a. anger
   - ☐ b. sickness
   - ☐ c. happiness

8. Once he let himself go, thinking this way, there was no bottom to the feeling of <u>betrayal</u>.
   - ☐ a. envy
   - ☐ b. love
   - ☐ c. desertion

✎ _____ **Number of correct answers**
Enter this number on the Vocabulary graph on page 134.

Personal Response

Do you think running away is a good solution to Tony's problems? Explain why or why not.

_____

_____

_____

_____

What would you do if you were in Tony's situation?

_____

_____

_____

_____

17 | How to Be Somebody

by Shirley Dever

Whenever something important needs to be done, many of us often have the tendency to let somebody else do it. In this selection, the author tells why it is important for each of us to be that somebody.

Three brothers had a fun evening together. One of them put a couple of pieces of alder on the fire in the wood stove before they went to bed. A couple of hours later, the fire was out of control. In their groggy state the brothers didn't know what to do. One panicked and jumped out a second-story window. Another, with amazing calmness, found his way to a door and got out OK. Later, the firefighters discovered the third boy by a bedroom window. He had died of smoke inhalation.

"Didn't anyone try to get him out?" And the same answer was given, again and again. "We thought *somebody else* went in to help him!"

An unknown author wrote a clever and brief story about this sort of thinking:

"This is the story about four people named Everybody, Somebody, Anybody, and Nobody. There was an important job to be done, and Everybody was sure that Somebody would do it. Anybody could have done it, but Nobody did it. Somebody got angry about that, because it was Everybody's job. Everybody thought Anybody could do it, but Nobody realized that Everybody wouldn't do it. It ended up that Everybody blamed Somebody when Nobody did what Anybody could have done."

Do you rely upon a mysterious "they" you refer to as Somebody Else? It's amazing how most of us rely on this unidentifiable person on a regular basis. We say, "I'm sorry I left the house open, but I figured Somebody Else would lock up." Nobody else did.

What is at stake is owning up to responsibility. And this simply means the ability to respond. Each of us is responsible for his own actions. We are also responsible for those times we do nothing in the face of needs.

Not to decide is to count on Somebody Else's taking over the responsibility you were to assume. It is to turn your back on the fact that life itself requires daily decisions. Life is a decision-making process. Not to decide is a cop-out.

Young people might be astounded to learn that wars were actually fought, for the most part, by young men still in their teens! Louis XIV of France did not think it surprising to have fourteen-year-old lieutenants in his armies. The oldest soldier in one of his corps was under the age of eighteen. Joan of Arc, the Maid of Orleans, led the French to a momentous victory at Orleans when she was seventeen and became a martyr at age nineteen.

Over and over again young people who refuse to cop out are consumed by purposes bigger than themselves. Then their inner cry becomes, "What can I do?" not, "What will Somebody Else do for me?"

John F. Kennedy made a statement, "Ask not what your country can do for you—ask what you can do for your country." This is the philosophy that breaks the Somebody Else dependency. Ask, "What can I do for that person who can use my help?"

Once I responded to the plea of a paraplegic girl who had a deep desire to go to

Hawaii. When I made sixty phone calls in her behalf, thirty-eight people responded with various amounts of money. Within a week I was staring in amazement at checks totaling one thousand dollars. It was a miracle! What I didn't know at the time I helped this young girl was that she would die one year after her dream trip!

Many Somebody Elses helped me, to be sure. But someone had to make those calls and take care of the details. After that experience, it has been easier to rely on myself rather than those mysterious "theys" who are all around me.

Most of you wish to be in control of your life more than you are. Releasing your dependence on other people is a great way to gain more control and to feel better about yourself.

Instead of saying, "I need Somebody Else to get me started," motivate yourself by saying, "I have a self-starter; I'll use it!" Or rather than saying, "Somebody Else has so much going for him/her," say to yourself, "I have special gifts, too, and I'm going to use them."

You are Somebody. You have certain talents and gifts. You can do certain things that not just Anybody can do. Nobody can put you down or discourage you unless you let him/her. So is Somebody Else really so important after all? ■

✔ Enter your reading time below. Then look up your reading speed on the Words-per-Minute table on page 130.

Reading Time   _____

Reading Speed   _____

Enter your reading speed on the Reading Speed graph on page 131.

Comprehension

Put an **X** in the box next to the correct answer for each question or statement. Do not look back at the selection.

1. The third brother caught in the fire
   - ☐ a. was burned to death.
   - ☐ b. died of smoke inhalation.
   - ☐ c. died when he jumped out of a second-story window.

2. Who did everyone think had gone in to help get the third brother out?
   - ☐ a. one of the other brothers
   - ☐ b. somebody else
   - ☐ c. one of the firemen

3. In the brief story by the unknown author, who did the job that had to be done?
   - ☐ a. Nobody
   - ☐ b. Somebody
   - ☐ c. Everybody

4. We are responsible not only for our own actions but for the times when we
   - ☐ a. make hasty decisions.
   - ☐ b. ask others for help.
   - ☐ c. do nothing in the face of needs.

5. Wars have actually been fought for the most part by
   - ☐ a. men between the ages of 25 and 45.
   - ☐ b. professional soldiers.
   - ☐ c. young men in their teens.

6. Joan of Arc became a martyr at the age of
   - ☐ a. 19.
   - ☐ b. 17.
   - ☐ c. 24.

7. The author raised money to send the paraplegic girl to Hawaii by
   - ☐ a. hiring someone to raise the money.
   - ☐ b. making an appeal on television.
   - ☐ c. making 60 phone calls.

74

8. Who said, "Ask not what your country can do for you—ask what you can do for your country"?
   - [ ] a. John F. Kennedy
   - [ ] b. Ronald Reagan
   - [ ] c. Robert F. Kennedy

✎ _____ Number of correct answers
Enter this number on the Comprehension graph on page 132.

Critical Thinking

Put an **X** in the box next to the best answer for each question or statement. You may look back at the selection if you'd like.

1. The author wrote this selection to
   - [ ] a. entertain you.
   - [ ] b. depress you.
   - [ ] c. inspire you.

2. Which of the following statements best expresses the main idea of the selection?
   - [ ] a. People should take control of their own lives by being responsible for their own actions and not relying on others.
   - [ ] b. Everyone has certain talents and gifts and should have the confidence to use them.
   - [ ] c. Young people are more concerned about themselves than about bigger purposes.

3. Which word best describes a person who is in control of his or her own life?
   - [ ] a. dependent
   - [ ] b. responsible
   - [ ] c. friendly

4. The author thinks people should each take responsibility because
   - [ ] a. she doesn't want to do it.
   - [ ] b. no one else will.
   - [ ] c. then people will regain control over their own lives.

5. The third boy died as a result of the fire because
   - [ ] a. everyone thought somebody else went in to help him.
   - [ ] b. he couldn't find his way out because of the smoke.
   - [ ] c. he panicked and jumped out a window.

6. Which of the following is a statement of opinion rather than fact?
   - [ ] a. Once I responded to the plea of a paraplegic girl who had a deep desire to go to Hawaii.
   - [ ] b. Most of you wish to be in control of your life more than you are.
   - [ ] c. Joan of Arc, the Maid of Orleans, led the French to a momentous victory at Orleans when she was 17.

7. Which of the following does *not* fit with the other two?
   - [ ] a. John F. Kennedy
   - [ ] b. Joan of Arc
   - [ ] c. Louis XIV of France

8. Compared to the teens that fought in wars long ago, young people today are more
   - [ ] a. responsible.
   - [ ] b. irresponsible.
   - [ ] c. scared.

✎ _____ Number of correct answers
Enter this number on the Critical Thinking graph on page 133.

Vocabulary

Each numbered sentence contains an underlined word or phrase from the selection. Following are three definitions. Put an **X** in the box next to the best meaning of the word as it is used in the sentence.

1. In their <u>groggy</u> state the brothers didn't know what to do.
   - ☐ a. happy
   - ☐ b. filthy
   - ☐ c. sleepy

2. Do you rely upon a <u>mysterious</u> "they" you refer to as Somebody Else?
   - ☐ a. magic
   - ☐ b. unknown
   - ☐ c. absent

3. What is at stake is <u>owning up</u> to responsibility.
   - ☐ a. buying
   - ☐ b. admitting
   - ☐ c. denying

4. Young people might be <u>astounded</u> to learn that wars were actually fought, for the most part, by young men still in their teens!
   - ☐ a. shocked
   - ☐ b. pleased
   - ☐ c. interested

5. Joan of Arc led the French to a <u>momentous</u> victory at Orleans.
   - ☐ a. brief
   - ☐ b. loud
   - ☐ c. great

6. Over and over again young people who refuse to cop out are <u>consumed</u> by purposes bigger than themselves.
   - ☐ a. deeply involved
   - ☐ b. quickly forgotten
   - ☐ c. easily bored

7. Releasing your <u>dependence</u> on other people is a great way to gain more control and to feel better about yourself.
   - ☐ a. anger
   - ☐ b. frustration
   - ☐ c. reliance

8. Instead of saying, "I need Somebody Else to get me started," <u>motivate</u> yourself by saying, "I have a self-starter."
   - ☐ a. deceive
   - ☐ b. encourage
   - ☐ c. threaten

✎ _____ **Number of correct answers**
Enter this number on the Vocabulary graph on page 134.

Personal Response

Do you think young people today are more likely to say, "What can I do?" or "What will Somebody Else do for me?" Explain.

_____

_____

_____

_____

18 | Sounder

by William H. Armstrong

Sounder is the story of a poor sharecropper's son and the dog he loves. In this passage from the book, the boy makes a sad visit and also worries about his missing dog.

The boy moved quickly around the corner and out of sight of the iron door and the gray cement walls of the jail. At the wall in front of the courthouse he stood for a while and looked back. When he had come, he was afraid, but he felt good in one way because he would see his father. He was bringing him a cake for Christmas. And he wasn't going to let his father know he was grieved. So his father *wouldn't* be grieved.

There were only a few people loafing around the courthouse wall, so the boy sat for a spell. He felt numb and tired. What would he say to his mother? He would tell her that the jailer was mean to visitors but didn't say nothing to the people in jail. He wouldn't tell her about the cake. When he told her his father had said she shouldn't send him again, that he would send word by the visiting preacher, she would say, "You grieved him, child. I told you to be perk so you wouldn't grieve him."

Nobody came near where the boy sat or passed on the street in front of the wall. He had forgotten the most important thing, he thought. He hadn't asked his father where Sounder had come to him on the road when he wasn't more'n a pup. That didn't make any difference.

But along the road on the way to the jail, before the bull-necked man had ruined everything, the boy had thought his father would begin to think and say "If a stray ever follard you and it wasn't near a house, likely somebody's dropped it. So you could fetch it home and keep it for a dog."

"Wouldn't do no good now," the boy murmured to himself. If he found a stray on the way home, his mother would say "I'm afraid, child. Don't bring it in the cabin. If it's still here when mornin' comes, you take it down the road and scold it and run so it won't foller you no more. If somebody come lookin', you'd be in awful trouble."

A great part of the way home the boy walked in darkness. In the big houses he saw beautiful flickering lights and candles in the windows. Several times dogs rushed to the front gates and barked as he passed. But no stray pup came to him along the lonely, empty stretches of road. In the dark he thought of the bull-necked man crumpled on the floor in the cake crumbs, like the strangled bull in the cattle chute, and he walked faster. At one big house the mailbox by the road had a lighted lantern hanging on it. The boy walked on the far side of the road so he wouldn't show in the light. "People hangs 'em out when company is comin' at night," the boy's father had once told him.

When court was over, they would take his father to a road camp or a quarry or a state farm. Would his father send word with the visiting preacher where he had gone? Would they take his father away to the chain gang for a year or two years before he could tell the visiting preacher? How would the boy find him then? If he lived closer to the town, he could watch each day, and when they took his father away in the wagons where convicts were penned up in huge wooden crates, he could follow.

The younger children were already in bed when the boy got home. He was glad, for they would have asked a lot of questions that might make his mother feel bad, questions like "Is everybody chained up in jail? How long do people stay in jail at one time?"

The boy's mother did not ask hurtful questions. She asked if the boy got in all right and if it was warm in the jail. The boy told her that the jailer was mean to visitors but that he didn't say nothing to the people in jail. He told her he heard some people singing in the jail.

"Sounder ain't come home?" the boy said to his mother after he had talked about the jail. He had looked under the porch and called before he came into the cabin.

Now he went out, calling and looking around the whole cabin. He started to light the lanterns to look more, but his mother said "Eat your supper." ■

✔ Enter your reading time below. Then look up your reading speed on the Words-per-Minute table on page 130.

    Reading Time   _____

    Reading Speed   _____

Enter your reading speed on the Reading Speed graph on page 131.

Comprehension

Put an **X** in the box next to the correct answer for each question or statement. Do not look back at the selection.

1. Whom did the boy go to see at the jail?
   - ☐ a. the visiting preacher
   - ☐ b. his father
   - ☐ c. the judge

2. What had the boy brought to the jail?
   - ☐ a. his dog
   - ☐ b. a book
   - ☐ c. a cake

3. What had the boy decided to tell his mother about the jail?
   - ☐ a. The jailer was mean to visitors but didn't say nothing to the people in the jail.
   - ☐ b. The jailer was mean to the people in the jail but didn't say nothing to visitors.
   - ☐ c. He wasn't allowed to go into the jail.

4. The most important thing he had wanted to ask his father was
   - ☐ a. where Sounder had come to him.
   - ☐ b. if he would be home for Christmas.
   - ☐ c. where they were going to send him when court was over.

5. On the boy's way home, the road was
   - ☐ a. bright.
   - ☐ b. crowded and busy.
   - ☐ c. dark and lonely.

6. On his way home, the boy walked on the far side of the road
   - ☐ a. because he was afraid of the barking dogs.
   - ☐ b. so he wouldn't show up in the light.
   - ☐ c. because he was hopeful of finding a stray pup.

7. Why was the boy glad the younger children were in bed when he got home?
   - ☐ a. They would have asked questions that might make his mother feel bad.
   - ☐ b. He didn't want to have to play with them.
   - ☐ c. They annoyed him.

8. After he got home, the boy started to look for
   - ☐ a. his dog, Sounder.
   - ☐ b. his mother.
   - ☐ c. one of the younger children.

✎ _____ Number of correct answers
Enter this number on the Comprehension graph on page 132.

Critical Thinking

Put an ✗ in the box next to the best answer for each question or statement. You may look back at the selection if you'd like.

1. The main purpose of the first paragraph is to let you know the boy was
   - ☐ a. visiting his father who was in jail.
   - ☐ b. bringing his father a Christmas cake.
   - ☐ c. afraid to go to the jail.

2. What kind of mood or feeling does the author create in this story?
   - ☐ a. exciting
   - ☐ b. cheerful
   - ☐ c. sad

3. What was the boy hoping to find on the road as he walked home?
   - ☐ a. money
   - ☐ b. a stray pup
   - ☐ c. a lighted lantern

4. The boy's longing for a dog shows that he is
   - ☐ a. spoiled.
   - ☐ b. demanding.
   - ☐ c. lonely.

5. The boy wished he lived closer to town so that he
   - ☐ a. could watch each day, and follow the wagon when his father was moved.
   - ☐ b. would not have as far to walk when he visited his father.
   - ☐ c. could get a job to help his mother.

6. The fact that the boy did not want his father to "be grieved" shows
   - ☐ a. his fear of the jail.
   - ☐ b. his love for his father.
   - ☐ c. his hope for his father's freedom.

7. What did the boy do just before he talked about the jail to his mother?
   - ☐ a. ate his supper
   - ☐ b. started to light a lantern to take outside
   - ☐ c. looked for his dog, Sounder

8. Which sentence correctly restates the following: "If it's still here when mornin' comes, you take it down the road and scold it and run so it won't foller you no more. If somebody come lookin', you'd be in trouble."
   - ☐ a. If it's here in the morning, chase it away because you could get in trouble if somebody found it here.
   - ☐ b. If it's still here in the morning, don't scold it or you could get in trouble if somebody finds out.
   - ☐ c. If it's still here in the morning, chase it away so anyone looking for it won't be able to follow it.

✎ _____ Number of correct answers
Enter this number on the Critical Thinking graph on page 133.

Vocabulary

Each numbered sentence below contains an underlined word from the selection. Following are three definitions. Put an ✗ in the box next to the best meaning of the word as it is used in the sentence.

1. And he wasn't going to let his father know he was <u>grieved</u>. So his father *wouldn't* be <u>grieved</u>.
   - ☐ a. very sad
   - ☐ b. very angry
   - ☐ c. very thrilled

2. There were only a few people <u>loafing</u> around the courthouse wall, so the boy sat for a spell.
   - ☐ a. reading newspapers
   - ☐ b. relaxing and doing nothing
   - ☐ c. waiting for someone

3. He felt <u>numb</u> and tired.
   - ☐ a. proud
   - ☐ b. happy
   - ☐ c. stunned

4. The bull-necked man had <u>ruined</u> everything.
   - ☐ a. brought home
   - ☐ b. spoiled
   - ☐ c. made possible

5. "Wouldn't do no good now," the boy <u>murmured</u> to himself.
   - ☐ a. shouted loudly
   - ☐ b. said firmly
   - ☐ c. spoke softly

6. In the big houses he saw beautiful <u>flickering</u> lights and candles in the windows.
   - ☐ a. dying
   - ☐ b. many-colored
   - ☐ c. blinking

7. In the dark he thought of the bull-necked man <u>crumpled</u> on the floor.
   - ☐ a. sleeping soundly
   - ☐ b. creeping around
   - ☐ c. in a twisted heap

8. "If it's still there when mornin' comes, you take it down the road and <u>scold</u> it and run so it won't foller you no more."
   - ☐ a. talk angrily at
   - ☐ b. laugh at
   - ☐ c. hide from

✎ _____ **Number of correct answers**
Enter this number on the Vocabulary graph on page 134.

Personal Response

I know how the boy felt when he could not find his pet dog because

_____

_____

The boy and his family are very poor in material things. Can you think of something important that they do have?

_____

_____

19 | She Wanted to Read

by Ella Kaiser Carruth

Mary McLeod Bethune was a black educator who spent her whole life working for the improvement of educational opportunities for black students. In this passage from the book She Wanted to Read, a biography of Bethune, Mary starts a school for poor black children.

Henry Flagler was building a railroad all the way down the east coast of Florida, from Jacksonville to Miami. He was employing Negro workers because they were cheap. A great many of them were in Daytona. Most of them had children. They were living in shacks worse than those in The Terry in Augusta. The children were running wild in the streets. Mary seemed to hear a voice say, "That is the place. Build your school there."

Her husband, Albertus, wasn't so sure about her school. He thought Palatka was a pretty good place for them to live. Mary listened but she never gave up her idea. She knew that if she went to Daytona, Albertus would come too.

One day she begged a ride for herself and her little boy with a family that was going to Daytona. It was only seventy miles away. But in 1904 the sand was deep on Florida roads. Practically no one had an automobile—certainly not the poor family that gave Mary and little Albert a ride. So it was three dusty days after they left Palatka before they reached Daytona. There Mary hunted up the only person she knew, and she and little Albert stayed with this friend for a few days.

As she had done in The Terry in Augusta, Mary walked up and down the poor streets of Daytona. She was looking for two things—a building for the school she was determined to start and some pupils for that school.

After a day or two, she found an empty shack on Oak Street. She thought this would do. The owner said she could rent it for $11.00 a month. But it wasn't worth that much. The paint had peeled off, the front steps wobbled so that she had to hang onto the shaky railing to keep from falling, the house was dirty, it had a leaky roof. In most of the windows the panes of glass were broken or cracked.

Eleven dollars a month! Mary said she only had $1.50. She promised to pay the rent as soon as she could earn the money. The owner trusted her. By the time she was sure she could have the building, she had five little girls from the neighborhood as her pupils.

What a school! A rickety old house and five little girls!

The little girls pitched in and cleaned the house. The neighbors helped with scrubbing brushes, brooms, hammers, nails, and saws. Soon the cottage could be lived in, but there were no chairs, no tables, no beds. There was no stove. However, there were no pots and pans to cook in, even if there had been a stove.

Mary set about changing these things. She found things in trash piles and the city dump. Nobody but Mrs. Bethune would have thought of making tables and chairs and desks from the old crates she picked up and brought home. Behind the hotels on the beach she found cracked dishes, old lamps, even some old clothes. She took them home too. Everything was scoured and mended and used. "Keep things clean and neat" was her motto then; and as long as she lived the pupils in her school had to live up to that motto. She found a piece of gay cretonne and made a ruffled skirt of it to brighten up the packing box she used for her own desk.

Her little pupils had no pencils. They wrote with charcoal slivers made from burned logs. Their ink was elderberry juice. What good was ink or a pencil if there was no paper to write on? Mrs. Berthune took care of that too.

Every time she went to the store to get a little food, or a few pots and pans, she had each article wrapped separately. The pieces of wrapping paper were carefully removed and smoothed out. The little girls used this paper to write their lessons with their charcoal pencils.

She needed a cookstove very badly but she couldn't pay for one. What should she do? Her little pupils had to have warm food.

Unexpectedly, the problem was solved for her. One day a wrinkled old white neighbor said to her, "Can you read?"

Mary said, "Yes."

"Then will you read me this letter from my son? I can't find my glasses."

Mary read the letter to her.

"Thanks," said the mother.

Mary turned to go. "You're welcome."

The old woman stood by her open door and thought a moment. Then she said, "I got an old cookstove. 'Tain't doin' me a mite o' good. Would you want it?" ■

✔ Enter your reading time below. Then look up your reading speed on the Words-per-Minute table on page 130.

Reading Time _____

Reading Speed _____

Enter your reading speed on the Reading Speed graph on page 131.

Comprehension

Put an **X** in the box next to the correct answer for each question or statement. Do not look back at the selection.

1. Henry Flagler employed Negro workers because
   - ☐ a. he wanted to help them.
   - ☐ b. they were cheap.
   - ☐ c. they were the only ones who would work.

2. Mary started her school in
   - ☐ a. Daytona.
   - ☐ b. Augusta.
   - ☐ c. Palatka.

3. In what year did Mary move to the city where she started her school?
   - ☐ a. 1984
   - ☐ b. 1904
   - ☐ c. 1934

4. How much money did Mary have for the rent?
   - ☐ a. $150.00
   - ☐ b. $15.00
   - ☐ c. $1.50

5. Mary found the first group of pupils for her school
   - ☐ a. by advertising in the newspaper.
   - ☐ b. from across town.
   - ☐ c. in her own neighborhood.

6. Mary began her school with
   - ☐ a. eleven pupils.
   - ☐ b. seven pupils.
   - ☐ c. five pupils.

7. Why did Mary dig through trash piles?
   - ☐ a. She was looking for something she had lost.
   - ☐ b. She was looking for things she could use at her school.
   - ☐ c. She was looking for things she could use in her home.

8. How did Mary get the cookstove she needed?
   - ☐ a. She found one in the city dump.
   - ☐ b. She bought a used one.
   - ☐ c. An old woman offered her one.

✎ _____ **Number of correct answers**
Enter this number on the Comprehension graph on page 132.

Critical Thinking

Put an **✗** in the box next to the best answer for each question or statement. You may look back at the selection if you'd like.

1. Which choice best describes this story?
   - ☐ a. a story of a real person's life written by someone else
   - ☐ b. a story of a real person's life written by that person
   - ☐ c. a story made up by the author using imagination and creativity

2. The best title for this passage from the book *She Wanted to Read* is
   - ☐ a. "Mary Moves to Daytona."
   - ☐ b. "Mary Begins a New Career."
   - ☐ c. "Mary Starts a New School."

3. How did Mary's husband, Albertus, feel about going to Daytona?
   - ☐ a. He was strongly in favor.
   - ☐ b. He was a little reluctant.
   - ☐ c. He was against it.

4. Where did Mary and her family live just before they moved to Daytona?
   - ☐ a. Palatka
   - ☐ b. Augusta
   - ☐ c. Jacksonville

5. Mary's pupils used elderberry juice to write with because
   - ☐ a. it doesn't stain like ink does.
   - ☐ b. they couldn't afford ink.
   - ☐ c. it's easier to write with than ink.

6. Which of the following is a statement of opinion rather than fact?
   - ☐ a. Henry Flagler was building a railroad from Jacksonville to Miami.
   - ☐ b. The owner said she could rent it for $11.00 a month.
   - ☐ c. Nobody but Mrs. Bethune would have thought of making tables and chairs and desks from the old crates.

7. Which of the following does *not* fit with the other two?
   - ☐ a. Miami
   - ☐ b. Daytona
   - ☐ c. Palatka

8. The word that best describes Mary McLeod Bethune is
   - ☐ a. poor
   - ☐ b. determined
   - ☐ c. neat

✎ _____ **Number of correct answers**
Enter this number on the Critical Thinking graph on page 133.

Vocabulary

Each numbered sentence contains an underlined word from the selection. Following are three definitions. Put an **X** in the box next to the best meaning of the word as it is used in the sentence.

1. He was <u>employing</u> Negro workers because they were cheap.
   - ☐ a. avoiding
   - ☐ b. hiring
   - ☐ c. mistreating

2. <u>Practically</u> no one had an automobile—certainly not the poor family that gave Mary and little Albert a ride.
   - ☐ a. almost
   - ☐ b. honestly
   - ☐ c. usually

3. She was looking for two things—a building for the school she was <u>determined</u> to start and some pupils for that school.
   - ☐ a. wishing
   - ☐ b. sure
   - ☐ c. unwilling

4. What a school! A <u>rickety</u> house and five little girls!
   - ☐ a. sturdy
   - ☐ b. noisy
   - ☐ c. flimsy

5. Everything was <u>scoured</u> and mended and used.
   - ☐ a. repaired
   - ☐ b. scrubbed
   - ☐ c. scratched

6. "Keep things clean and neat" was her <u>motto</u> then.
   - ☐ a. level
   - ☐ b. ideal
   - ☐ c. saying

7. They wrote with charcoal <u>slivers</u> made from burned logs.
   - ☐ a. lumps
   - ☐ b. slices
   - ☐ c. powder

8. <u>Unexpectedly</u>, the problem was solved for her.
   - ☐ a. regularly
   - ☐ b. easily
   - ☐ c. surprisingly

✐ _____ **Number of correct answers**
Enter this number on the Vocabulary graph on page 134.

Personal Response

Mary McLeod Bethune spent her whole life trying to provide her students with the best education possible. What are three good reasons for getting the best education you can?

_____

_____

Which of the three reasons you've listed above is the most important? Explain why you think so.

_____

_____

20 | The Birth of the Blues

by Henry and Melissa Billings

Can you imagine life without blue jeans? Before Levi Strauss solved an unusual clothing problem almost 150 years ago, there were no blue jeans.

Nothing is more American than a pair of blue jeans. At one time only Americans wore them. The fashion has long since spread around the world. Still, blue jeans remain a popular symbol of America. They didn't begin as a fashion statement, however. They began as a practical solution to a specific problem.

In 1849 gold was discovered in California. That news sparked the famous California Gold Rush. Thousands of "forty-niners" rushed to the gold fields hoping to find their fortune. A few miners did strike it rich. But most did not. They spent whatever money they made on lodging, food, clothing, picks, and shovels. Clothing was a particular problem. The miners spent long days kneeling in dirt, scrambling over rocks, and squatting in water. Under these conditions, pants wore out quickly. Miners complained about how easily their pants ripped or the seams pulled out. As one miner put it, "pants don't wear worth a hoot up in the diggin's."

According to legend, one miner mentioned this problem to a merchant named Levi Strauss. Strauss had been born in Germany in 1829. At the age of 17, he came to America and settled in New York City. There he worked in his brother's store selling dry goods such as shirts, blankets, pillows, and underwear. In 1853 Levi Strauss sailed to San Francisco to make his fortune. He planned to make his money not by panning for gold, but by running a store. He figured he could sell all sorts of dry goods to miners. Strauss even brought some canvas with him.

He thought the material would make good tents or wagon covers.

After hearing the miners' clothing complaints, though, Strauss changed his mind. He used the canvas to make up some pants for miners. Calling them "waist-high overalls," he sold them for 22 cents a pair. The miners loved "those pants of Levi's" or "Levi's" for short. One miner even sat in a watering trough until his Levi's shrank to a perfect fit. The brown pants were homely, but they wore like iron.

Strauss sold his pants as fast as he could make them. Still, he constantly worked to improve his product. He switched from canvas to French denim, a cotton twill material even stronger and more durable than canvas. Later he also changed his dye color to a dark indigo blue. Because of the new color, some people began to call their Levi's "blue denims" or "blue jeans." (The word *jeans* comes from the name of a city in Italy also associated with denim pants—Genoa.)

But there was still one major problem with the Levi's. The pants themselves never ripped, but sometimes the seams did. This was especially true in areas of stress such as the pockets. Miners often stuffed samples of ore in their pockets. The pressure frequently ripped open the pockets. In 1872 a tailor named Jacob Davis came up with a brilliant idea. He was tired of sewing up the same pockets over and over again. So Davis put copper rivets on the corners of the pockets and at the base of the fly. It worked. The seams didn't rip anymore.

Davis lacked the money to patent his process. So he wrote to Levi Strauss and suggested that they form a partnership. Strauss agreed. A patent for the new process was issued on May 20, 1873. And so modern blue jeans were born. Before long, Levi Strauss & Company became the largest clothing manufacturer in the world.

Strauss had intended to make simple work pants. But his blue jeans became immensely popular for all-around use far beyond the gold fields. Men and women in all walks of life enjoyed them. *Vogue* magazine featured women in Levi's as early as 1935. Lana Turner, a famous movie star, had her blue jeans studded with diamonds.

The rivets on the rear pockets, though, did not last. When children began wearing blue jeans to school, the rivets scratched the school chairs and desks. Teachers complained. So in 1937 the rivets on the rear pockets were taken out. They were replaced by extra heavy stitching.

Later, blue jeans became a hot item in communist nations. In the old Soviet Union, for instance, they sold for as much as $140 a pair on the black market. In some communist nations, blue jeans were even used as a form of money. So it may be that communism fell not because the United States had better weapons but because we had better pants! ■

✔ **Enter your reading time below. Then look up your reading speed on the Words-per-Minute table on page 130.**

Reading Time _____

Reading Speed _____

Enter your reading speed on the Reading Speed graph on page 131.

Comprehension

Put an **X** in the box next to the correct answer for each question or statement. Do not look back at the selection.

1. Gold was discovered in California in
   - ☐ a. 1849.
   - ☐ b. 1897.
   - ☐ c. 1927.

2. Where did Levi Strauss open his own dry goods store?
   - ☐ a. New York City
   - ☐ b. San Francisco
   - ☐ c. Los Angeles

3. Although Strauss first made his pants from canvas, he soon switched to
   - ☐ a. linen.
   - ☐ b. blue denim.
   - ☐ c. wool.

4. The word *jeans* comes from Genoa, a city in
   - ☐ a. Germany.
   - ☐ b. the Soviet Union.
   - ☐ c. Italy.

5. How did Jacob Davis make the pockets of Levi's stronger?
   - ☐ a. by sewing all the pocket seams twice
   - ☐ b. by making them from a stronger material
   - ☐ c. by putting copper rivets in the corners of the pockets

6. Levi Strauss and Jacob Davis
   - ☐ a. became partners.
   - ☐ b. sued one another.
   - ☐ c. tried to put each other out of business.

7. Women wearing Levi's were featured in *Vogue* magazine as early as
   - ☐ a. 1873.
   - ☐ b. 1935.
   - ☐ c. 1947.

8. Blue jeans became a hot item in
   - ☐ a. South American countries.
   - ☐ b. communist nations.
   - ☐ c. Asian nations.

✎ _____ Number of correct answers
Enter this number on the Comprehension graph on page 132.

Critical Thinking

Put an **X** in the box next to the best answer for each question or statement. You may look back at the selection if you'd like.

1. The main purpose of the first paragraph is to
   - ☐ a. explain how Levi Strauss invented blue jeans.
   - ☐ b. describe the first blue jeans.
   - ☐ c. introduce you to the topic of the selection.

2. Which statement below best expresses the main idea of the selection?
   - ☐ a. Some items of clothing can be both practical and fashionable.
   - ☐ b. Levi's became so popular around the world that they sometimes sold for as much as $140 in the old Soviet Union.
   - ☐ c. Blue jeans were created by Levi Strauss to fill the needs of California gold miners and have since become popular worldwide.

3. From this selection, you can conclude that
   - ☐ a. Levi Strauss's main goal in making changes to his pants was to make them more stylish.
   - ☐ b. Levi Strauss was a good businessman.
   - ☐ c. blue jeans are not very popular among women.

4. Based on what you've read in this selection, you can predict that probably
   - ☐ a. blue jeans will continue to be popular among both men and women for many years to come.
   - ☐ b. blue jeans will continue to be popular only among men.
   - ☐ c. the popularity of blue jeans will soon begin to fade away.

5. The forty-niners were dissatisfied with their pants because the pants
   - ☐ a. ripped too easily.
   - ☐ b. weren't attractive enough.
   - ☐ c. were too expensive.

6. Which of the following is a statement of opinion rather than fact?
   - ☐ a. Levi Strauss sold his waist-high overalls for 22 cents a pair.
   - ☐ b. Blue jeans look old-fashioned today.
   - ☐ c. Levi Strauss was born in Germany.

7. Which word best describes Strauss's first "waist-high overalls"?
   - ☐ a. comfortable
   - ☐ b. expensive
   - ☐ c. practical

8. Choose the sentence that correctly restates the following sentence from the selection: "The pants were homely, but they wore like iron."
   - ☐ a. Even though the pants weren't attractive, they lasted a long time.
   - ☐ b. The pants were very stiff and uncomfortable.
   - ☐ c. The pants were so ugly that no one wanted to wear them outside.

✎ _____ Number of correct answers
Enter this number on the Critical Thinking graph on page 133.

Vocabulary

Each numbered sentence contains an underlined word from the selection. Following are three definitions. Put an **✗** in the box next to the best meaning of the word as it is used in the sentence.

1. That news <u>sparked</u> the famous California Gold Rush.
   - ☐ a. delayed
   - ☐ b. started
   - ☐ c. stopped

2. The miners spent long days kneeling in dirt, scrambling over rocks, and <u>squatting</u> in water.
   - ☐ a. wading
   - ☐ b. swimming
   - ☐ c. crouching

3. After hearing the miners' clothing <u>complaints</u>, Strauss changed his mind.
   - ☐ a. requests
   - ☐ b. findings of fault
   - ☐ c. needs

4. The brown pants were <u>homely</u>, but they wore like iron.
   - ☐ a. ugly
   - ☐ b. large
   - ☐ c. beautiful

5. He switched from canvas to French denim, a cotton twill material even stronger and more <u>durable</u> than canvas.
   - ☐ a. uncomfortable
   - ☐ b. colorful
   - ☐ c. lasting

6. Miners often stuffed samples of ore in their pockets. The <u>pressure</u> frequently ripped open the pockets.
   - ☐ a. force
   - ☐ b. hardness
   - ☐ c. sharpness

7. But his blue jeans became <u>immensely</u> popular for all-around use.
   - ☐ a. extremely
   - ☐ b. fortunately
   - ☐ c. barely

8. Lana Turner, a famous movie star, had her blue jeans <u>studded</u> with diamonds.
   - ☐ a. stripped or made bare
   - ☐ b. shortened
   - ☐ c. decorated

✎ _____ **Number of correct answers**
Enter this number on the Vocabulary graph on page 134.

Personal Response

Why do you think blue jeans have been popular for so long all over the world?

_____

_____

_____

✔ **Check Your Progress**
Study the graphs you completed for Lessons 11–20 and answer the How Am I Doing? questions on page 136.

21 | Song of the Stranger

by Angela Tung

Thirteen-year-old Karen Nomura's relationship with her Obasan—the Japanese name for grandmother—is not a happy one. In fact, Karen can't stand her! Now she has to spend two months with Obasan in a strange land. In this passage, Karen has just arrived at her grandmother's house in Japan.

I looked around. Slowly I became more and more awake.

So I was here. I turned in a slow circle. Everything was pale wood and very clean. Nothing was out of place. Through the porch doors I could see the yard slope down to a line of trees. It was quiet except for the ticking of a clock somewhere. I sat down at the table. I was alone. I was thousands and thousands of miles away from everyone that I knew. I pressed my hands against my cheeks and felt my eyes starting to tear.

Then the voice of Mrs. Prettyman, my art teacher, said in my head, *Make the most of it.* I sat up straight. *Keep painting*, my mother's voice said. I wiped my eyes and stood. I was here and there was nothing I could do about it, except to make it good. I picked up my things and went down the hall.

Like the kitchen, my room was clean and spare. The floor was carpeted, but there was nothing on the walls except for a long scroll with Chinese characters that hung over the frameless bed. From movies I'd seen I knew that people in Japan often slept on a futon on the floor. The only other piece of furniture was a small dresser in the corner.

At least I had my own room, I told myself. I had my own space to do my own thing. I could close the door. I began to unpack.

Soon I had all my clothes put away in the dresser and closet. On top of the dresser I put the picture of me and my friends, along with the travel journal I had been keeping. I found some tape in one of the kitchen drawers and used it to stick Mrs. Prettyman's poster up on the wall across from the bed. Around it I taped my other photos. I wasn't sure where I'd put my canvases yet. I'd have to get some sort of makeshift easel. In the meantime, I had my sketchbook. I settled down on the floor with that and my paint kit.

As I continued to work on the drawing of my mother, I left my paint kit open beside me, just so that I could see the tubes of oils and acrylics—some wrinkled and pinched, others smooth and brand new—the fat and skinny brushes, the soft colors of the water paints. With all of these familiar things around me, I started to feel less homesick.

I was putting the final details into the sketch when I noticed that the room had grown considerably darker and that the sunlight hitting the wall by the dresser was now bright orange. I set my sketch pad aside and went to the window. On this side of the house, the land ran down to a small stream and all around were trees, full and green. The sun was a giant crimson ball that hung low in the distance. It seemed farther away here than at home, as though the sky were bigger. It was strange not to see any houses in the near distance. A chill came over me, though it wasn't a bad chill.

"So you decide to ruin my wall?"

I jumped and turned around.

Obasan stood in the doorway, pointing at the poster and photos on the wall. Her face was in shadow, so I couldn't see her expression.

"They're not ruining the wall, Obasan. It's just tape."

"You think tape does not ruin the wall? It tears off the paint, it leaves marks." She stepped into the room. "And what is that?"

She was peering into my paint kit. *Oh, no,* I thought. *I should have hidden it.*

Before I could answer she said, "Did you think you could paint in this room?"

"I wasn't painting, Obasan. I was just—"

"I do not want to see you painting in this room." She turned away from the kit as if it were a rat. "Put it in the basement. Put all your painting things in the basement. I do not want to see any of them. And take those things off my wall. Immediately." She turned and disappeared into the darkness of the hall.

I slumped onto the floor. So I didn't really have my own room, my own space. *Make the most of it,* Mrs. Prettyman said. *Keep painting,* my mother said. How could I? I wanted to ask them. How could I? ■

✔ Enter your reading time below. Then look up your reading speed on the Words-per-Minute table on page 130.

Reading Time _____

Reading Speed _____

Enter your reading speed on the Reading Speed graph on page 131.

Comprehension

Put an **X** in the box next to the correct answer for each question or statement. Do not look back at the selection.

1. This story takes place in
   □ a. China.
   □ b. Japan.
   □ c. the United States.

2. Mrs. Prettyman is Karen's
   □ a. mother.
   □ b. grandmother.
   □ c. art teacher.

3. Karen learned that people in Japan often sleep on a futon on the floor from
   □ a. movies.
   □ b. Obasan.
   □ c. her travel journal.

4. Karen decided there was nothing she could do about her situation except to
   □ a. make it good.
   □ b. go home.
   □ c. move out of Obasan's home.

5. Karen was finishing a drawing of
   □ a. Obasan.
   □ b. the sunset.
   □ c. her mother.

6. By having her own room, Karen felt that she at least had
   □ a. a place to write in her journal.
   □ b. a place to talk to her mother by telephone.
   □ c. her own space to do her own thing.

7. Obasan fears that Karen will
   □ a. want to go home.
   □ b. ruin the wall.
   □ c. make too much noise.

8. Where does Obasan want Karen to put her painting things?
   □ a. in the basement
   □ b. in the kitchen
   □ c. in her room

✎ _____ Number of correct answers
Enter this number on the Comprehension graph on page 132.

Critical Thinking

Put an ✘ in the box next to the best answer for each question or statement. You may look back at the selection if you'd like.

1. What mood or feeling does the author create in this story?
   - ☐ a. loneliness
   - ☐ b. happiness
   - ☐ c. excitement

2. Who is the narrator of this story?
   - ☐ a. Obasan
   - ☐ b. an outside observer
   - ☐ c. Karen

3. From this selection, you can conclude that Obasan
   - ☐ a. is very concerned about neatness.
   - ☐ b. enjoys having a guest in her house.
   - ☐ c. is a pleasant old woman.

4. What word best describes how Karen feels?
   - ☐ a. excited
   - ☐ b. homesick
   - ☐ c. curious

5. Obasan becomes upset with Karen because Karen
   - ☐ a. put her paint kit in the basement.
   - ☐ b. put tape on the wall.
   - ☐ c. put her clothes in the dresser and closet.

6. Which of the following is a statement of opinion rather than fact?
   - ☐ a. I was thousands and thousands of miles away from everyone that I knew.
   - ☐ b. It seemed farther away here than at home, as though the sky were bigger.
   - ☐ c. Through the porch doors I could see the yard slope down to a line of trees.

7. Which event happened last?
   - ☐ a. Karen taped a poster and pictures on the wall.
   - ☐ b. Karen almost finished a drawing she was doing in her sketchbook.
   - ☐ c. Karen put her clothes away in the dresser and closet.

8. The relationship between Karen and Obasan is best described as
   - ☐ a. warm.
   - ☐ b. close.
   - ☐ c. distant.

✎ _____ **Number of correct answers**
Enter this number on the Critical Thinking graph on page 133.

Vocabulary

Each numbered sentence contains an underlined word from the selection. Following are three definitions. Put an ✘ in the box next to the best meaning of the word as it is used in the sentence.

1. Everything was <u>pale</u> wood and very clean.
   - ☐ a. dark
   - ☐ b. shiny
   - ☐ c. light-colored

2. The floor was carpeted, but there was nothing on the walls except for a long <u>scroll</u> with Chinese characters that hung over the frameless bed.
   - ☐ a. painting
   - ☐ b. wall lamp
   - ☐ c. roll of paper

3. Like the kitchen, my room was clean and <u>spare</u>.
   - ☐ a. extra
   - ☐ b. lightly furnished
   - ☐ c. completely furnished

4. On top of the dresser I put the picture of me and my friends, along with the travel <u>journal</u> I had been keeping.
   - ☐ a. daily record
   - ☐ b. passport
   - ☐ c. map

5. I'd have to get some sort of <u>makeshift</u> easel.
   - ☐ a. permanent
   - ☐ b. easily carried
   - ☐ c. temporary

6. As I continued to work on the drawing of my mother, I left my paint kit open beside me, just so that I could see the tubes of oils and <u>acrylics</u>.
   - ☐ a. pastes
   - ☐ b. paints
   - ☐ c. glue

7. I was putting the final details into the <u>sketch</u> when I noticed the room had grown considerably darker.
   - ☐ a. paint kit
   - ☐ b. book
   - ☐ c. drawing

8. Her face was in shadow, so I couldn't see her <u>expression</u>.
   - ☐ a. staring eyes
   - ☐ b. look that shows feeling
   - ☐ c. way of standing

✐ _____ **Number of correct answers**
Enter this number on the Vocabulary graph on page 134.

Personal Response

I can understand how Karen feels because

_____

_____

_____

If you were Karen, what would you say to Obasan to make things better between the two of you?

_____

_____

_____

22 | Skin: The Bag You Live In

by Linda Allison

Blood and Guts is a book full of fascinating information and drawings that describe how the inside of your body works. This passage tells about the marvelous container that protects you and the inside of your body: your skin.

The first creatures on earth were sea creatures. They were protected from the sun's rays by a blanket of ocean. Under water they remained cool and moist. The seas they swam were rich in nutrients and minerals. The skin that separated them from their outside world was rather simple, since their insides were very much like their outsides.

Since the earliest days, our environment and our skins have changed considerably. Inside your body, cells live bathed in a fluid environment much like the ancient seas. Outside your body's skin is air, a gaseous space, full of drying winds and radiation from the sun. A dangerous environment for a creature who is sixty percent water.

Your skin's main job is to serve as a watertight container, preventing your internal sea from drying up. Skin also keeps things out. Skin provides protection from bacteria, dirt, and the sun's rays.

Skin is an important part of your body's climate control system. Sweating, goose bumps, and simple heat loss from the skin all help keep your internal temperature comfortable. Skin is also a sensor; thousands of nerve endings in the skin keep you informed of events outside.

Mammals, warm-blooded creatures like ourselves, are very fussy about their internal temperatures, and with good reason. A few degrees can mean the difference between life and death.

A very important job for the bag you live in is to make sure its contents are kept at a comfortable temperature. Skin does this two ways: by radiation and by evaporation. When your internal temperature rises, your brain signals your blood to step up circulation to the skin. In this way, the body's internal heat is carried by the blood to the surface, where it is lost by radiation. Meanwhile, the sweat glands spring into action, and perspiration is released through the pores. This liquid evaporates on your skin, and you cool off. When your temperature drops, your brain signals that heat must now be saved. Less blood circulates to the skin, and sweating stops.

Suppose you had a hot can of Coke. If you leave it alone, it will cool down. That's radiation. If you're in a hurry for it to cool, you could cover it with a damp cloth. That's evaporation.

On a humid day the air is already full of water and is unwilling to accept more. The perspiration on your skin tends to stay on your skin rather than evaporating into the air. Eighty percent humidity means the air contains eighty percent of the water it can hold. At this humidity your cooling system has slowed down and is operating at about twenty percent efficiency. No wonder you're sticky and warm!

Skin is made up of layers, rather like a birthday cake. The under layer is called the *dermis.* It is alive and contains blood vessels, glands, nerve cells, and hair roots. The layer on top is the *epidermis,* the skin's outer limits. This is made up of layers of dead cells.

Skin cells in the dermis are constantly growing and being pushed to the surface. There they die and form the dead outer layer. The dead outer cells are rubbed off in little bits. In this way your skin reconstructs itself every few weeks.

If your skin is punctured with a round instrument like a nail, it leaves a hole. However, it doesn't leave a round hole. It leaves a slit. Surgeons have made maps of these slit patterns, or cleavage lines. They generally follow the crease marks on the skin and are about the same for most bodies. Skin that is cut along a cleavage line rather than across has a much less likely chance of leaving a scar.

Your skin lies between you and the outside world. It is in a position to tell you a lot about what is going on out there. It does so with a vast network of nerve endings that sit just under your tough outside hide. Touch is no simple sense. You are able to feel warm, squishy, furry, hard, slimy, freezing cold, greasy, hot, etc. Your skin is equipped with sensors for heat, cold, pressure, and pain.

Sensations are often combinations of two or more kinds of information. Getting kissed is a combination of pressure and heat. Getting kicked is a combination of pressure and pain.

Your skin is a suit with many surfaces. It is damp, dry, thick, thin, hairy, and smooth. It is pleated to give you room to move. It's the last word in all-purpose suits. ∎

✔ Enter your reading time below. Then look up your reading speed on the Words-per-Minute table on page 130.

    Reading Time   _____

    Reading Speed   _____

Enter your reading speed on the Reading Speed graph on page 131.

Comprehension

Put an **X** in the box next to the correct answer for each question or statement. Do not look back at the selection.

1. What were the first creatures on earth?
   - ☐ a. land creatures
   - ☐ b. flying creatures
   - ☐ c. sea creatures

2. The human body is
   - ☐ a. 60 percent skin.
   - ☐ b. 60 percent water.
   - ☐ c. 40 percent skin.

3. The skin's main job is to
   - ☐ a. keep the bones in place.
   - ☐ b. serve as a watertight container.
   - ☐ c. replace water loss.

4. When the body's internal heat is carried by blood to the surface, it is lost by
   - ☐ a. radiation.
   - ☐ b. humidity.
   - ☐ c. evaporation.

5. In mammals, a difference of a few degrees in their internal body temperatures can mean the difference between
   - ☐ a. a faster or slower circulation.
   - ☐ b. being wet or dry.
   - ☐ c. life or death.

6. If you cover a hot can of Coke with a damp cloth to speed up its cooling, you have an example of
   - ☐ a. radiation.
   - ☐ b. evaporation.
   - ☐ c. circulation.

7. Surgeons generally cut along crease marks on the skin because
   - ☐ a. less blood circulates there.
   - ☐ b. the skin is easier to cut that way.
   - ☐ c. there is a much smaller chance of leaving a scar.

8. Sensations are often combinations of two or more kinds of information. Getting kicked is a combination of pain and
   - ☐ a. pressure.
   - ☐ b. heat.
   - ☐ c. cold.

✎ _____ Number of correct answers
Enter this number on the Comprehension graph on page 132.

Critical Thinking

Put an ✗ in the box next to the best answer for each question or statement. You may look back at the selection if you'd like.

1. The author's purpose in mentioning a can of Coke was to
   - ☐ a. provide an example of radiation and evaporation.
   - ☐ b. show that she understands other things besides science.
   - ☐ c. appeal to readers who drink it.

2. Which statement best expresses the main idea of the selection?
   - ☐ a. Skin is an important part of the body's climate control system, keeping its internal temperature comfortable.
   - ☐ b. The skin's main job is to keep the inside of the body from drying up.
   - ☐ c. Since the earliest days, our environment and our skins have changed considerably.

3. The author says that mammals are warm blooded. What does that mean?
   - ☐ a. They are emotional creatures.
   - ☐ b. Their blood is naturally warm by itself.
   - ☐ c. They have an internal temperature control.

4. The author says that skin is "the last word in all-purpose suits." This means that skin
   - ☐ a. has many jobs.
   - ☐ b. comes in many colors.
   - ☐ c. is washable.

5. Humidity makes you feel hotter because sweat
   - ☐ a. evaporates very quickly when it's humid.
   - ☐ b. evaporates very slowly when it's humid.
   - ☐ c. radiates quickly when it's humid.

6. The *dermis* contains
   - ☐ a. layers of dead skin.
   - ☐ b. slit patterns, or cleavage lines.
   - ☐ c. constantly growing skin cells.

7. What happens when blood circulation to the skin is increased?
   - ☐ a. The body heats up.
   - ☐ b. The blood stops moving.
   - ☐ c. The body cools down.

8. Which of the following does *not* fit with the other two?
   - ☐ a. humidity
   - ☐ b. epidermis
   - ☐ c. perspiration

✎ _____ Number of correct answers
Enter this number on the Critical Thinking graph on page 133.

Vocabulary

Each numbered sentence contains an underlined word from the selection. Following are three definitions. Put an ✗ in the box next to the best meaning of the word as it is used in the sentence.

1. Since the earliest days, our environment and our skins have changed <u>considerably</u>.
   ☐ a. quite a bit
   ☐ b. not very much
   ☐ c. differently

2. Your skin's main job is to serve as a watertight container, preventing your <u>internal</u> sea from drying up.
   ☐ a. warm
   ☐ b. outer
   ☐ c. inner

3. When your internal temperature rises, your brain signals your blood to step up <u>circulation</u> to the skin.
   ☐ a. movement
   ☐ b. amount
   ☐ c. increase

4. It is <u>pleated</u> to give you room to move.
   ☐ a. folded
   ☐ b. checkered
   ☐ c. soft

5. The <u>perspiration</u> on your skin tends to stay on your skin rather than evaporating into the air.
   ☐ a. humidity
   ☐ b. circulation
   ☐ c. sweat

6. In this way your skin <u>reconstructs</u> itself every few weeks.
   ☐ a. remembers
   ☐ b. requests
   ☐ c. rebuilds

7. It does so with a <u>vast</u> network of nerve endings that sit just under your tough outside hide.
   ☐ a. skinny
   ☐ b. large
   ☐ c. speedy

8. On a <u>humid</u> day the air is already full of water and is unwilling to accept more.
   ☐ a. hot
   ☐ b. damp
   ☐ c. cloudy

✎ _____ Number of correct answers
Enter this number on the Vocabulary graph on page 134.

Personal Response

What was the most surprising or interesting thing you learned in this selection about the skin?

_____

_____

When I think about my skin, I wonder why

_____

_____

23 | Seward's Warning

by Natalie Babbitt

To some the sea is a source of beauty and pleasure. It is even a place to make a living. To others it is a source of tragedy and heartache. In this passage from The Eyes of the Amaryllis, a young man tells what he thinks the meaning of the sea is.

Listen, all you people lying lazy on the beach, is this what you imagine is the meaning of the sea? Oh, yes, it winks and sparkles as it sways beside you, spreading lacy foam along the sand, as dainty as a handkerchief. But can you really think that is all it means? The foam, and these tender cowrie shells as pearly as a baby's toes? This purple featherweed floating up fine as the plume of an ostrich? That child in yellow, her face so grave beneath the brim of her linen hat? She sits there filling her bright tin bucket with those tiny shovelsful of sand, as cautious as a pharmacist measuring a dose, and watching her, you murmur to each other, "Sweet! How Sweet!"

But listen. This is not the meaning of the sea. Less than a hundred and fifty years ago, on this very spot, out there where that row of rocky points thrusts up above the swells, a ship was lost. There, see? Where those herring gulls are wheeling down? It all looks much the same today: the rocks, and this beach that narrows to a pathway when the tide is in. But on that day at summer's end, the sky went dark, like twilight, with a shrieking wind, and the sea rose up tall as trees. Out there, where the gulls sit sunning now, it flung a ship against the rocks and swallowed her. It swallowed her whole, and every member of her crew. Captain, cargo, every inch of sail and rigging, gone in a single gulp, while the captain's wife stood helpless, watching. Up there, on that little bluff, that's where she stood, shrieking back at the wind,

her son gone dumb with horror at her side. And there was nothing to bury afterwards. Nothing. The sea had taken it all, and gave back not one plank or shred of canvas.

That is part of the meaning. But there's more. A little later, three months or four, a young man broke his heart over a foolish girl. Nothing to remark about in that, you think. But he was an artist, that young man. He had carved a figurehead for the *Amaryllis*, the ship that was swallowed, carved it in the likeness of the captain's wife—proud and handsome, with long red hair. Then he up and broke his heart over a foolish girl, and one morning very early, while the mist was still thick, he climbed into a dinghy and rowed himself straight out, out there well past the place where that sailboat skims along. He rowed out early in the morning, and he vanished. Oh, they found the dinghy later, just here, washed up, its oars stowed neat and dry inside. But he was not washed up, though they searched the shore for days. He was swallowed, they said at last, swallowed like the *Amaryllis*.

But he was not quite swallowed. Listen. That is the rest of the meaning of the sea. You lie here so unthinking—have you forgotten that the surface of the earth is three-fourths water? Those gulls out there, they know it better than you. The sea can swallow ships, and it can spit out whales upon the beach like watermelon seeds. It will take what it wants, and it will keep what it has taken, and you may not take away from it what it does not wish to give. Listen. No matter how old you grow or how important on the land, no matter how powerful or beautiful or rich, the sea does not care a straw for you. That frail grip you keep on the wisp of life that holds you upright—the sea can turn it loose in an instant. For life came first from the sea and can be taken back. Listen. Your bodies, they are three-fourths water, like the surface of the earth. Ashes to ashes, the Bible says, and maybe so—but the ashes float on the water of you, like that purple featherweed floating on the tide. Even your tears are salt.

You do not listen. What if I told you that I was that carver of figureheads, the one they said was swallowed by the sea? The breeze in your ears, it carries my voice. But you only stretch on your fluffy towels and talk of present things, taking the sea for granted. So much the worse for you, then. ■

✔ Enter your reading time below. Then look up your reading speed on the Words-per-Minute table on page 130.

Reading Time _____

Reading Speed _____

Enter your reading speed on the Reading Speed graph on page 131.

Comprehension

Put an **X** in the box next to the correct answer for each question or statement. Do not look back at the selection.

1. To whom is the narrator speaking?
   - ☐ a. himself
   - ☐ b. the captain's wife
   - ☐ c. the people lying on the beach

2. During the storm that caused the shipwreck, the sea rose
   - ☐ a. as tall as trees.
   - ☐ b. as high as a man.
   - ☐ c. many, many feet.

3. Who stood beside the captain's wife on the bluff as she watched his ship go down?
   - ☐ a. the young man that carved figureheads
   - ☐ b. her son
   - ☐ c. her daughter

4. The *Amaryllis* was the name of the
   - ☐ a. young girl.
   - ☐ b. captain's wife.
   - ☐ c. lost ship.

5. How long after the shipwreck did the young man row out to sea in a dinghy?
   - ☐ a. about a year
   - ☐ b. three or four weeks
   - ☐ c. three or four months

6. How much of the earth's surface is covered with water?
   - ☐ a. one-fourth
   - ☐ b. one-half
   - ☐ c. three-fourths

7. The young man who carved figureheads
   - ☐ a. vanished.
   - ☐ b. sailed on the *Amaryllis*.
   - ☐ c. ran away in the storm.

8. The narrator points out that people's tears are like the sea in that they both
   - ☐ a. are wet.
   - ☐ b. contain salt.
   - ☐ c. are hard to control.

✎ _____ Number of correct answers
Enter this number on the Comprehension graph on page 132.

Critical Thinking

Put an ✗ in the box next to the best answer for each question or statement. You may look back at the selection if you'd like.

1. What mood or feeling does the author create in this story?
   - ☐ a. hopeful
   - ☐ b. depressing
   - ☐ c. comforting

2. Who is the narrator of this story?
   - ☐ a. the woman who lost her husband at sea
   - ☐ b. an outside observer
   - ☐ c. the young man who carved the figurehead and was lost at sea

3. Which of the following statements best expresses the main idea of the selection?
   - ☐ a. The meaning of the sea is not sandy beaches and fun; it means power and danger.
   - ☐ b. Many people have been lost at sea.
   - ☐ c. It is especially dangerous to sail in stormy weather.

4. Why weren't there any debris or bodies after the wreck?
   - ☐ a. The ship really sailed away.
   - ☐ b. A magic spell was cast on the ship.
   - ☐ c. The sea is so huge that it can make things disappear.

5. What caused the young man to row out to sea early one morning?
   - ☐ a. He was broken-hearted over a foolish girl.
   - ☐ b. He was going fishing.
   - ☐ c. He thought it would help him to carve the figurehead of a ship if he saw where the *Amaryllis* went down.

6. Which of the following is a statement of opinion rather than fact?
   - ☐ a. But listen. This is not the meaning of the sea.
   - ☐ b. Your bodies, they are three-fourths water.
   - ☐ c. Out there, where the gulls sit sunning now, it flung a ship against the rocks and swallowed her.

7. According to the narrator, the sea is best described as being
   - ☐ a. huge.
   - ☐ b. predictable.
   - ☐ c. uncaring.

8. The feeling the author expresses in this selection is
   - ☐ a. hope.
   - ☐ b. anger.
   - ☐ c. sorrow.

✎ _____ Number of correct answers
Enter this number on the Critical Thinking graph on page 133.

Vocabulary

Each numbered sentence contains an underlined word from the selection. Following are three definitions. Put an ✗ in the box next to the best meaning of the word as it is used in the sentence.

1. Oh, yes, it winks and sparkles as it sways beside you, spreading lacy foam along the sand, as <u>dainty</u> as a handkerchief.
   - ☐ a. delicate
   - ☐ b. white
   - ☐ c. crumpled

2. That child in yellow, her face so <u>grave</u> beneath the brim of her linen hat?
   - ☐ a. bright
   - ☐ b. gay
   - ☐ c. serious

3. She sits there filling her bright tin bucket with those tiny shovelsful of sand, as <u>cautious</u> as a pharmacist measuring a dose.
   - ☐ a. happy
   - ☐ b. careful
   - ☐ c. grim

4. There, see? Where those herring gulls are <u>wheeling</u> down?
   - ☐ a. circling
   - ☐ b. diving
   - ☐ c. screaming

5. Up there . . . that's where she stood, shrieking back at the wind, her son gone <u>dumb</u> with horror at her side.
   - ☐ a. insane
   - ☐ b. silent
   - ☐ c. dizzy

6. Oh, they found the dinghy later, just here, washed up, its oars <u>stowed</u> neat and dry inside.
   - ☐ a. loose
   - ☐ b. left
   - ☐ c. stored

7. That <u>frail</u> grip you keep on the wisp of life that holds you upright—the sea can turn it loose in an instant.
   - ☐ a. strong
   - ☐ b. thoughtless
   - ☐ c. weak

8. But you only stretch on your fluffy towels and talk of present things, taking the sea for <u>granted</u>.
   - ☐ a. pleasure and fun
   - ☐ b. accepted as it appears
   - ☐ c. mysterious and unknown

✎ _____ **Number of correct answers**
Enter this number on the Vocabulary graph on page 134.

Personal Response

I understand how the narrator feels because

_____

_____

_____

What do you think is the "meaning" of the sea?

_____

_____

_____

24 A Long Way to Whiskey Creek

by Patricia Beatty

A Long Way to Whiskey Creek tells the story of a boy's adventure in the Old West. In this passage from the book, the boy, with the help of a cowboy friend, is trying to get away from someone.

There was no sound but the chink of the harness as Pilgrim and Hooraw followed the wagon ruts northward. Parker glanced once or twice at Nate Graber as they went along, wondering if he'd made a mistake. Maybe he should a picked somebody else to keep him company. Take that bus'ness of not hiding in back with the coffin. Nate should a done that for his own good. It was beginnin' to look like this Graber kid didn't know a heifer from a horned frog—even if he did come from Texas.

Before long they came to the Colorado River, flowing eastward. Parker turned off the road, jolting the wagon to a spot under some trees. Here he stopped the team. "We'll cross over in the mornin'," he said.

Nate nodded his head, his pale ringlets fluttering in the chilly night wind. "You think nobody will be coming after me until then?" he asked.

Parker only grunted. Just as soon as he could get his hands on some shears, he was going to do something about Graber's hair. "Did the widow make you have them curls? You hanker after keepin' 'em?"

"I hate them!"

Parker laughed as he started to unhitch the horses. He'd tie them to the wagon wheel, not hobble them tonight. There wasn' any point in chasin' after 'em at daybreak, not if they wanted a real head start on somebody the widow might be sendin'. Maybe she'd never find out which way Nate'd lit out or who he'd gone with. Parker was almost willing to bet his precious Lone Star boots that few men who might have seen them leaving Cottonwood would tell on Nate.

"There's some cornbread and some slab bacon in one a them sacks, kid," he told Nate. "We ain't makin' no fire tonight. We'll be sleepin' under the wagon."

"All right, Parker." Nate Graber threw his blankets and Parker's bedroll onto the grass, and asked, "How far is the next town?"

"That'd be Lockville. Thirty miles north, I reckon. I ain't never been there. I ain't never been outa this county or north a this river. I don' even know where this here river goes."

"Oh, it flows to the Gulf of Mexico. It rises in West Texas," Nate said precisely. Then he added, "How long will we be gone?"

"I dunno. Six weeks—two months. That oughta give ya time to have a rest from the widow, huh?"

Nate spoke eagerly. "That would give me time to teach you to read and write, Parker. I helped teach the smaller children at school, so I know how."

From the wagon wheel where he was tying the team, Parker said, "I can't see a man needs it to be a roughstring rider."

"Everybody ought to be able to do those things!" protested Nate Graber.

"I told you I can't see no need for it to herd cow brutes or bust broncs. Don't keep at me about it unless you want your wishbone scratched up plenty." Before Nate could say anything else, Parker started whistling for J. E. B. Stuart. He'd tie him up, too. There wasn' any call for the dog to be out chasin' jacks two nights in a row.

They forded the Colorado at daybreak at what Parker judged was the most shallow place. The water came high enough on the wheels for Nate to reach down nervously and touch it.

"Is it warmer'n it was when we got baptized in it?" asked Parker.

"A little bit." Nate sighed with relief as the team plodded onto the opposite bank. "I thought for a while there the water would flood the wagon and maybe your team would have to swim."

Parker shook his head. "Nope. I reckoned right about this ford and didn' git us into no boghole. But there'll be a couple more rivers to cross before we git where I'm goin'." He certainly hadn't liked Nate's nervousness at this first fording. "You know what it means in Texas when somebody says 'He's a good man to ride a river with'?"

"No."

Parker Quiney sighed. "I didn't reckon ya would. It means you got pure grit in ya. There ain't nothin more dangerous than ridin' rivers with a trail herd." He clucked to Hooraw and Pilgrim as they reached high ground. Wet from his swim, J. E. B. Stuart went dashing past the team. Parker asked, "Nate, what'd your pa do anyhow?"

"Oh, he was a schoolteacher. . . ."

Parker groaned aloud. "A wisdom bringer. I mighta knowed it." ■

✔ Enter your reading time below. Then look up your reading speed on the Words-per-Minute table on page 130.

Reading Time   _____

Reading Speed   _____

Enter your reading speed on the Reading Speed graph on page 131.

Comprehension

Put an **X** in the box next to the correct answer for each question or statement. Do not look back at the selection.

1. Parker and Nate were trying to get away from
   - ☐ a. cattle rustlers.
   - ☐ b. the town sheriff.
   - ☐ c. the widow.

2. Parker wants some shears to
   - ☐ a. trim Nate's long hair.
   - ☐ b. clean his Lone Star boots.
   - ☐ c. mend the wagon wheel.

3. How long did Parker expect that they would be gone?
   - ☐ a. about a year
   - ☐ b. six weeks to two months
   - ☐ c. four to six months

4. Nate wants to teach Parker how to
   - ☐ a. be a roughstring rider.
   - ☐ b. hobble horses.
   - ☐ c. read and write.

5. Who was J. E. B. Stuart?
   - ☐ a. another roughstring rider
   - ☐ b. Parker's horse
   - ☐ c. Parker's dog

6. What river did Parker and Nate ford?
   - ☐ a. the Missouri River
   - ☐ b. the Mississippi River
   - ☐ c. the Colorado River

7. According to Parker, what does it mean in Texas when somebody says, "He's a good man to ride a river with"?
   - ☐ a. He's a good swimmer.
   - ☐ b. He's got pure grit in him.
   - ☐ c. He's familiar with the river.

8. Nate's father had been a
   - ☐ a. schoolteacher.
   - ☐ b. preacher.
   - ☐ c. roughstring rider.

✎ _____ Number of correct answers
Enter this number on the Comprehension
graph on page 132.

Critical Thinking

Put an ✗ in the box next to the best answer
for each question or statement. You may look
back at the selection if you'd like.

1. The author tells this story mainly by
   - ☐ a. retelling personal experiences.
   - ☐ b. using her imagination and
     creativity.
   - ☐ c. telling two stories about the same
     topic.

2. Who is the narrator of this story?
   - ☐ a. Nate Graber
   - ☐ b. Parker Quiney
   - ☐ c. an outside observer

3. How does Parker feel about having Nate
   with him on the trail?
   - ☐ a. He thinks Nate will be helpful with
     the horses.
   - ☐ b. He's glad to have his company.
   - ☐ c. He's not sure it's a good idea.

4. The word that best describes Parker's
   attitude about Nate's offer is
   - ☐ a. uninterested.
   - ☐ b. pleased.
   - ☐ c. enthusiastic.

5. Parker drove the wagon through the river
   because
   - ☐ a. it was the only way to cross.
   - ☐ b. they were being followed.
   - ☐ c. Nate was nervous.

6. Which of the following is a statement of
   opinion rather than fact?
   - ☐ a. "There's some cornbread and some
     slab bacon in one a them sacks,
     kid."
   - ☐ b. "There ain't nothing more
     dangerous than ridin' rivers with a
     trail herd."
   - ☐ c. "But there'll be a couple more
     rivers to cross before we git where
     I'm goin'."

7. Which of the following does not fit with
   the other two?
   - ☐ a. Parker Quiney
   - ☐ b. J. E. B. Stuart
   - ☐ c. Nate Graber

8. Which skill does Nate Graber think is
   most important?
   - ☐ a. knowing how to read and write
   - ☐ b. herding cows and busting broncs
   - ☐ c. driving wagons

✎ _____ Number of correct answers
Enter this number on the Critical Thinking
graph on page 133.

Vocabulary

Each numbered sentence contains an
underlined word from the selection.
Following are three definitions. Put an ✗ in
the box next to the best meaning of the word
as it is used in the sentence.

1. Parker turned off the road, jolting the
   wagon to a spot under some trees.
   - ☐ a. bouncing
   - ☐ b. steering
   - ☐ c. leading

2. Nate nodded his head, his pale <u>ringlets</u> fluttering in the chilly night wind.
   - ☐ a. rings
   - ☐ b. bells
   - ☐ c. curls

3. Just as soon as he could get his hands on some <u>shears</u>, he was going to do something about Graber's hair.
   - ☐ a. knives
   - ☐ b. scissors
   - ☐ c. curlers

4. Parker was almost willing to bet his <u>precious</u> Lone Star boots that few men would tell on Nate.
   - ☐ a. comfortable
   - ☐ b. valuable
   - ☐ c. antique

5. "Oh, it <u>flows</u> to the Gulf of Mexico. It rises in West Texas," Nate said precisely.
   - ☐ a. drips irregularly
   - ☐ b. returns yearly
   - ☐ c. moves easily

6. "Everybody ought to be able to do those things," <u>protested</u> Nate Graber.
   - ☐ a. objected
   - ☐ b. whined
   - ☐ c. agreed

7. They <u>forded</u> the Colorado at daybreak at what Parker judged was the most shallow place.
   - ☐ a. reached
   - ☐ b. crossed
   - ☐ c. swam

8. "I <u>reckoned</u> right about this ford and didn' git us into no boghole."
   - ☐ a. figured
   - ☐ b. remembered
   - ☐ c. hoped

✎ _____ **Number of correct answers**
Enter this number on the Vocabulary graph on page 134.

Personal Response

Parker doesn't think he needs to learn to read and write because he's a roughstring rider who just herds cows and busts broncs. What would you say to him to try to convince him that it's important that he learn to read and write?

_____

_____

_____

Would you like to have lived in the Old West? Explain why you would or would not.

_____

_____

_____

25 | Rescued Whales

by Andrew McPhee

Every year for some unknown reason, large numbers of whales run themselves aground and become stranded. Tragically, in most cases the whales die. This selection, however, tells of the first time a group of whales was rescued and later successfully released back into the ocean.

Scientists smiled as the three young whales swam through the ocean, flipping, jumping, and racing one another in circles. After spending seven months in a 60,000-gallon pool at the New England Aquarium, the whales were now free.

The pilot whales, Notch, Small, and Tag, had been staying at the aquarium ever since they were rescued after running aground. Although about 60 other whales died during that stranding, the young whales were saved and nursed back to health. After six months, the whales were released from a ship about 120 miles off the coast of Massachusetts.

When the three whales finally swam away from the ship, scientists on board cheered. The event marked the first time that a group of whales has been rescued, cared for, and released back into the wild.

No one knows what causes whales to become stranded. Some biologists think that gently sloping beaches may upset the whales' sonar systems. Whales detect schools of fish and other objects by bouncing sonar pulses off the objects. When a whale approaches a gently sloping beach, the sonar pulses may bounce away from the whale instead of toward it. The whale may run aground.

Other experts think a leader of a group of whales becomes ill and beaches itself. Because whales often band together, other whales soon follow, stranding themselves as well.

Storms may also play a role in the stranding. Other possibilities include the presence of local magnetic deposits that upset the ability of whales to navigate by Earth's magnetic field or too many female whales going too close to shore in search of food for their young.

When a stranding occurs, teams of scientists and volunteers try to quickly push the whales back into deeper water. Without water for support, a stranded whale may suffocate under its own weight. Its organs may be crushed.

Even when rescuers succeed in getting a whale into deeper water, they often watch helplessly as the whale turns around and beaches itself again.

When Notch, Small, and Tag were rescued, they were all less than two years old and were much smaller than stranded adults. The scientists weren't sure whether the whales would survive.

Small, the tiniest whale, was still too young to feed himself. Scientists placed a special feeding tube in Small's stomach to give him fluids. In a few weeks, Small started to eat on his own. Then, aquarium workers say, Small would eat so much food all at once that he often got a bellyache.

Tag never had that problem. Weighing 800 pounds when rescued, Tag was the largest of the three whales. Tag usually ate his own food, plus some of Notch's food. Workers sometimes had to keep Tag in a corner while Notch and Small ate their own meals.

The scientists had to be careful that the animals did not become too dependent upon humans. The young pilot whales were kept in an isolated pool and human contact was limited.

During the first month, the whales were fed on a regular schedule. In later months, the animals were given food at different times, because in the ocean, the whales would eat irregularly. To get the whales to learn to capture food themselves, live fish were put in the pool. Although young pilot whales normally learn to forage for fish with the help of their mothers, the motherless whales did capture live food on their own.

By June, the animals were 10 feet long. Big Tag had gained over 300 pounds and weighed over 1,100 pounds. Weighing the whales every month to see if they were eating enough was a major project. It took about an hour for 12 workers to weigh each whale. They had to use a forklift to put the whales on the scale.

Aquarium biologists decided that the whales were strong enough to go home. After a 12-hour journey from Boston out into the Atlantic, the ship found an area where dozens of pilot whales were swimming in small groups.

Workers lowered Notch overboard first. Workers then lowered a large wooden box that held Small and Tag and watched as the two whales slid into the ocean. After swimming near the boat for a while, all three whales swam off.

The three whales seem to have been adopted by a pod of whales say biologists who have been tracking them. Since being released, the whales have traveled over 1,200 miles. Now scientists hope the whales stay healthy and leave the beaches to the tourists. ■

✔ Enter your reading time below. Then look up your reading speed on the Words-per-Minute table on page 130.

Reading Time _____

Reading Speed _____

Enter your reading speed on the Reading Speed graph on page 131.

Comprehension

Put an **X** in the box next to the correct answer for each question or statement. Do not look back at the selection.

1. How long were the rescued whales at the New England Aquarium?
   - ☐ a. seven months
   - ☐ b. one year
   - ☐ c. three months

2. What kind of whales were they?
   - ☐ a. humpback
   - ☐ b. blue
   - ☐ c. pilot

3. What causes whales to be stranded?
   - ☐ a. They become confused.
   - ☐ b. No one knows for sure.
   - ☐ c. They develop breathing problems.

4. How many whales did the scientists save?
   - ☐ a. three
   - ☐ b. two
   - ☐ c. four

5. Whales detect objects by using their
   - ☐ a. sonar system.
   - ☐ b. keen eyesight.
   - ☐ c. exceptional hearing.

6. The scientists put live fish in the whales' pool to
   - ☐ a. study how they eat.
   - ☐ b. teach them how to hunt.
   - ☐ c. give them something to do.

7. The whales were released from a ship about 120 miles off the coast of
   - ☐ a. Rhode Island.
   - ☐ b. Connecticut.
   - ☐ c. Massachusetts.

8. After the whales were released, scientists
   - ☐ a. fed them at different times.
   - ☐ b. forgot about them and turned their attention to other rescued whales.
   - ☐ c. began tracking them.

✎ _____ Number of correct answers
Enter this number on the Comprehension graph on page 132.

Critical Thinking

Put an ✗ in the box next to the best answer for each question or statement. You may look back at the selection if you'd like.

1. The author's main purpose in writing this selection was to
   - ☐ a. describe the work of aquarium biologists at the New England Aquarium.
   - ☐ b. inform you about the problem of whale strandings and how biologists deal with them.
   - ☐ c. entertain you with a story about three young whales.

2. The young pilot whales were kept in an isolated pool with limited outside contact because
   - ☐ a. the scientists did not want them to become too dependent on humans.
   - ☐ b. the scientists did not want other sea animals to catch a disease from them.
   - ☐ c. they were too big for the aquarium's main pool.

3. Which of the following is the most important idea in the selection?
   - ☐ a. Whales in captivity must be kept isolated or they will become too dependent on humans.
   - ☐ b. With expert care, all rescued whales can be nursed back to good health.
   - ☐ c. No one knows what causes whales to become stranded. But when strandings occur, whales must be pushed back into deep water quickly or they will die.

4. Why were scientists not sure whether the whales would survive?
   - ☐ a. The whales were badly injured.
   - ☐ b. The whales were all under two years old.
   - ☐ c. Wild creatures often cannot survive in captivity.

5. From information in the selection, you can predict that the whales will probably
   - ☐ a. return to the aquarium.
   - ☐ b. run aground again.
   - ☐ c. stay with the pod.

6. Which of the following is a statement of opinion rather than fact?
   - ☐ a. When a whale approaches a gently sloping beach, the sonar pulses may bounce away from the whale instead of toward it.
   - ☐ b. No one knows what causes whales to become stranded.
   - ☐ c. Tag was the largest of the three whales.

7. Compared to the other two whales, Notch was the
   - ☐ a. largest one.
   - ☐ b. smallest one.
   - ☐ c. middle-sized one.

8. Which of the following does *not* fit with the other two?
   ☐ a. volunteers
   ☐ b. biologists
   ☐ c. scientists

✎ _____ **Number of correct answers**
Enter this number on the Critical Thinking graph on page 133.

Vocabulary

Each numbered sentence contains an underlined word from the selection. Following are three definitions. Put an **X** in the box next to the best meaning of the word as it is used in the sentence.

1. After <u>spending</u> seven months in a 60,000-gallon pool the whales were now free.
   ☐ a. buying
   ☐ b. staying
   ☐ c. costing

2. Whales <u>detect</u> schools of fish and other objects by bouncing sonar pulses off the objects.
   ☐ a. evade
   ☐ b. find
   ☐ c. move

3. Because whales often band together, other whales soon follow, <u>stranding</u> themselves.
   ☐ a. joining together
   ☐ b. running away
   ☐ c. running aground

4. Without water for support, a stranded whale may <u>suffocate</u> under its own weight.
   ☐ a. become smothered
   ☐ b. become flattened
   ☐ c. become enlarged

5. Scientists placed a special feeding tube in Small's stomach to give him <u>fluids</u>.
   ☐ a. vitamins
   ☐ b. fish
   ☐ c. liquids

6. The young pilot whales were kept in an <u>isolated</u> pool, and human contact was limited.
   ☐ a. remote
   ☐ b. cooled
   ☐ c. small

7. Although young pilot whales normally learn to <u>forage</u> for fish with the help of their mothers, the motherless whales did capture live food on their own.
   ☐ a. search
   ☐ b. swim
   ☐ c. call

8. The three whales seem to have been <u>adopted</u> by a pod of whales, say biologists who have been tracking them.
   ☐ a. attacked
   ☐ b. taken in
   ☐ c. followed

✎ _____ **Number of correct answers**
Enter this number on the Vocabulary graph on page 134.

Personal Response

A question I would like to ask aquarium biologists is

_____

_____

26 | The Black Cauldron

by Lloyd Alexander

In this passage from the book about the faraway and long-ago land of Prydain a stranger who claims to be a prince causes a commotion when he rides into the little farm of Dallben the enchanter.

Autumn had come too swiftly. In the northernmost realms of Prydain many trees were already leafless, and among the branches clung the ragged shapes of empty nests. To the south, across the river Great Avren, the hills shielded Caer Dallben from the winds, but even here the little farm was drawing in on itself.

For Taran, the summer was ending before it had begun. That morning Dallben had given him the task of washing the oracular pig. Had the old enchanter ordered him to capture a full-grown gwythaint, Taran would gladly have set out after one of the vicious winged creatures. As it was, he filled the bucket at the well and trudged reluctantly to Hen Wen's enclosure. The white pig, usually eager for a bath, now squealed nervously and rolled on her back in the mud. Busy struggling to raise Hen Wen to her feet, Taran did not notice the horseman until he had reined up at the pen.

"You, there! Pig-boy!" The rider looking down at him was a youth only a few years older than Taran. His hair was tawny, his eyes black and deep-set in a pale, arrogant face. Though of excellent quality, his garments had seen much wear, and his cloak was purposely draped to hide his threadbare attire. The cloak itself, Taran saw, had been neatly and painstakingly mended. He sat astride a roan mare, a lean and nervous steed speckled red and yellow, with a long, narrow head, whose expression was as ill-tempered as her master's.

"You, pig-boy," he repeated, "is this Caer Dallben?"

The horseman's tone and bearing nettled Taran, but he curbed his temper and bowed courteously. "It is," he replied. "But I am not a pig-boy," he added. "I am Taran, Assistant Pig-Keeper."

"A pig is a pig," said the stranger, "and a pig-boy is a pig-boy. Run and tell your master I am here," he ordered. "Tell him that Prince Ellidyr, Son of Pen-Llarcau. . ."

Hen Wen seized this opportunity to roll in another puddle. "Stop that, Hen!" Taran cried, hurrying after her.

"Leave off with that sow," Ellidyr commanded. "Did you not hear me? Do as I say, and be quick about it."

"Tell Dallben yourself!" Taran called over his shoulder, trying to keep Hen Wen from the mud. "Or wait until I've done with my work!"

"Mind your impudence," Ellidyr answered, "or you shall have a good beating for it."

Taran flushed. Leaving Hen Wen to do as she pleased, he strode quickly to the railing and climbed over. "If I do," he answered hotly, throwing back his head and looking at Ellidyr full in the face, "it will not be at *your* hands."

Ellidyr gave a scornful laugh. Before Taran could spring aside, the roan plunged forward. Ellidyr, leaning from the saddle, seized Taran by the front of the jacket. Taran flailed his arms and legs vainly. Strong as he was, he could not break free. He was pummeled and shaken until his teeth rattled.

Ellidyr then urged the roan into a gallop, hauled Taran across the turf to the cottage, and there, while chickens scattered in every direction, tossed him roughly to the ground.

The commotion brought Dallben and Coll outdoors. The Princess Eilonwy hurried from the scullery, her apron flying and a cookpot still in her hand. With a cry of alarm she ran to Taran's side.

Ellidyr, without troubling to dismount, called to the white-bearded enchanter. "Are you Dallben? I have brought your pig-boy to be thrashed for insolence."

"Tut!" said Dallben, unperturbed by Ellidyr's furious expression. "Whether he is insolent is one thing, and whether he should be thrashed is another. In either case, I need no suggestions from you."

"I am a Prince of Pen-Llarcau!" cried Ellidyr.

"Yes, yes, yes," Dallben interrupted with a wave of his brittle hand. "I am quite aware of all that and too busy to be concerned with it. Go, water your horse and your temper at the same time. You shall be called when you are wanted."

Ellidyr was about to reply, but the enchanter's stern glance made him hold his tongue. He turned the roan and urged her toward the stable.

Princess Eilonwy and the stout, baldheaded Coll, meantime, had been helping Taran pick himself up.

"You should know better, my boy, than to quarrel with strangers," said Coll good-naturedly.

"That's true enough," Eilonwy added. "Especially if they're on horseback and you're on foot." ∎

✔ Enter your reading time below. Then look up your reading speed on the Words-per-Minute table on page 130.

Reading Time   _____

Reading Speed   _____

Enter your reading speed on the Reading Speed graph on page 131.

Comprehension

Put an **X** in the box next to the correct answer for each question or statement. Do not look back at the selection.

1. Who was Hen Wen?
   - ☐ a. an old enchanter
   - ☐ b. a vicious winged creature
   - ☐ c. a white pig

2. When the horseman rode up, Taran was busy
   - ☐ a. trying to bathe the pig.
   - ☐ b. feeding the pig.
   - ☐ c. cleaning the pigsty.

3. Ellidyr was
   - ☐ a. a Prince of Caer Dallben.
   - ☐ b. a Prince of Pen-Llarcau.
   - ☐ c. the husband of Princess Eilonwy.

4. What did Ellidyr call Taran?
   - ☐ a. the Assistant Pig-Keeper
   - ☐ b. a sow
   - ☐ c. pig-boy

5. Compared to Taran, Ellidyr was
   - ☐ a. younger.
   - ☐ b. older.
   - ☐ c. the same age.

6. What was Dallben's reaction when Ellidyr told him Taran should be thrashed for insolence?
   - ☐ a. He was angry.
   - ☐ b. He was unperturbed.
   - ☐ c. He agreed with Ellidyr.

7. Who ran to Taran's side to assist him?
   - ☐ a. Princess Eilonwy
   - ☐ b. Dallben
   - ☐ c. Coll

8. Why didn't Ellidyr talk back to Dallben?
   - ☐ a. Dallben left right away.
   - ☐ b. Ellidyr didn't have anything to say.
   - ☐ c. Dallben's stern glance prevented him.

✎ _____ **Number of correct answers**
Enter this number on the Comprehension graph on page 132.

Critical Thinking

Put an **X** in the box next to the best answer for each question or statement. You may look back at the selection if you'd like.

1. The purpose of the first paragraph is to
   - ☐ a. inform you that Caer Dallben is a little farm in Prydain.
   - ☐ b. establish the setting, the time and place, of the story.
   - ☐ c. inform you that the story takes place in autumn.

2. Who is the narrator of this story?
   - ☐ a. an outside observer.
   - ☐ b. Taran
   - ☐ c. Dallben

3. The word that best describes Ellidyr is
   - ☐ a. carefree.
   - ☐ b. arrogant.
   - ☐ c. calm.

4. Taran's response to Ellidyr's words, "Mind your impudence, or you shall have a good beating for it," shows that Taran
   - ☐ a. is very proud.
   - ☐ b. is very frightened.
   - ☐ c. has a sense of humor.

5. Taran became angry because
   - ☐ a. the pig bit him.
   - ☐ b. he fell into the mud.
   - ☐ c. Ellidyr was rude to him.

6. Which of the following is a statement of opinion rather than fact?
   - ☐ a. "You should know better, my boy, than to quarrel with strangers."
   - ☐ b. "But I am not a pig-boy. I am Taran, Assistant Pig-Keeper."
   - ☐ c. The Princess Eilonwy hurried from the scullery, her apron flying and a cookpot still in her hand.

7. In what way are Taran and Ellidyr alike?
   - ☐ a. Both are hard workers.
   - ☐ b. Both are from a royal family.
   - ☐ c. Both are hot-headed.

8. How did Taran feel about the task given to him by Dallben?
   - ☐ a. eager to begin
   - ☐ b. reluctant to begin
   - ☐ c. too angry to begin

✎ _____ **Number of correct answers**
Enter this number on the Critical Thinking graph on page 133.

Vocabulary

Each numbered sentence contains an underlined word from the selection. Following are three definitions. Put an **X** in the box next to the best meaning of the word as it is used in the sentence.

1. The hills <u>shielded</u> Caer Dallben from the winds.
   - ☐ a. exposed
   - ☐ b. eroded
   - ☐ c. protected

2. As it was, he filled the bucket at the well and trudged <u>reluctantly</u> to Hen Wen's enclosure.
   - ☐ a. happily
   - ☐ b. unwillingly
   - ☐ c. easily

3. Though of excellent quality, his garments had seen much wear, and his cloak was purposely draped to hide his threadbare <u>attire</u>.
   - ☐ a. suitcase
   - ☐ b. saddle
   - ☐ c. clothing

4. The horseman's tone and bearing nettled Taran, but he <u>curbed</u> his temper.
   - ☐ a. loosened
   - ☐ b. relaxed
   - ☐ c. controlled

5. "Mind your <u>impudence</u>," Ellidyr answered, "or you shall have a good beating for it."
   - ☐ a. rudeness
   - ☐ b. courtesy
   - ☐ c. appearance

6. He was <u>pummeled</u> and shaken until his teeth rattled.
   - ☐ a. beaten
   - ☐ b. caressed
   - ☐ c. brushed

7. Ellidyr, without <u>troubling</u> to dismount, called to the white-bearded enchanter.
   - ☐ a. stopping
   - ☐ b. asking
   - ☐ c. bothering

8. Ellidyr was about to reply, but the <u>enchanter's</u> stern glance made him hold his tongue.
   - ☐ a. farmer's
   - ☐ b. magician's
   - ☐ c. horseman's

✎ _____ **Number of correct answers**
Enter this number on the Vocabulary graph on page 134.

Personal Response

I know how Taran felt because

_____

_____

What would you have said to Ellidyr if you had been Dallben?

_____

_____

27 | A Summer to Die

by Lois Lowry

The book A Summer to Die describes the problems of two sisters growing up together. In this passage both sisters are unhappy about having to share a room.

It was Molly who drew the line.

She did it with chalk—a fat piece of white chalk left over from when we lived in town, had sidewalks, and used to play hopscotch, back when we were both younger. That piece of chalk had been around for a long time. She fished it out of a little clay dish that I had made in last year's pottery class, where it was lying with a piece of string and a few paper clips and a battery that we weren't quite sure was dead.

She took the chalk and drew a line right on the rug. Good thing it wasn't a fuzzy rug or it never would have worked; but it was an old, worn, leftover rug from the dining room of our other house: very flat, and the chalk made a perfect white line across the blue— and then, while I watched in amazement (because it was unlike Molly, to be so angry), she kept right on drawing the line up the wall, across the wallpaper with its blue flowers. She stood on her desk and drew the line up to the ceiling, and then she went back to the other side of the room and stood on her bed and drew the line right up to the ceiling on that wall too. Very neatly. Good thing it was Molly who drew it; if I had tried, it would have been a mess, a wavy line and off center. But Molly is very neat.

Then she put the chalk back in the dish, sat down on her bed, and picked up her book. But before she started to read again, she looked over at me (I was still standing there amazed, not believing that she had drawn the line at all) and said, "There. Now be as much of a slob as you want, only keep your mess on your side. *This* side is *mine.*"

When we lived in town we had our own rooms, Molly and I. It didn't really make us better friends, but it gave us a chance to ignore each other more.

Funny thing about sisters. Well, about us, anyway; Dad says it's unacademic to generalize. Molly is prettier than I am, but I'm smarter than Molly. I want with my whole being to *be* something someday; I like to think that someday, when I'm grown up, people everywhere will know who I am, because I will have accomplished something important—I don't even know for sure yet what I want it to be, just that it will be something that makes people say my name, Meg Chalmers, with respect. When I told Molly that once, she said that what she wants is to be Molly Something Else, to be Mrs. Somebody, and to have her children, lots of them, call her "Mother," with respect, and that's all she cares about. She's content, waiting for that; I'm restless, and so impatient. She's sure, absolutely sure, that what she's waiting for will happen, just the way she wants it to; and I'm so uncertain, so fearful my dreams will end up forgotten somewhere, someday, like a piece of string and a paper clip lying in a dish.

Being both determined and unsure at the same time is what makes me the way I am, I think: hasty, impetuous, sometimes angry over nothing, often miserable about everything. Being so well sorted out in her own goals, and so assured of everything happening the way she wants and expects it to, is what makes Molly the way she is: calm, easygoing, self-confident, downright smug.

Sometimes it seems as if, when our parents created us, it took them two tries, two daughters, to get all the qualities of one whole, well-put-together person. More often, though, when I think about it, I feel as if they got those qualities on their first try, and I represent the leftovers. That's not a good way to feel about yourself, especially when you know, down in the part of you where the ambition is, where the dreams are, where the logic lies, that it's not true.

The hardest part about living in the same room with someone is that it's hard to keep anything hidden. I don't mean the unmatched, dirty socks or the fourteen crumpled papers with tries at an unsuccessful poem on them, although those are the things that upset Molly, that made her draw the line. I mean the parts of yourself that are private: the tears you want to shed sometimes for no reason, the thoughts you want to think in a solitary place, the words you want to say aloud to hear how they sound, but only to yourself. ∎

✔ Enter your reading time below. Then look up your reading speed on the Words-per-Minute table on page 130.

Reading Time   _____

Reading Speed   _____

Enter your reading speed on the Reading Speed graph on page 131.

Comprehension

Put an **X** in the box next to the correct answer for each question or statement. Do not look back at the selection.

1. Molly drew the line with
   - ☐ a. crayon.
   - ☐ b. chalk.
   - ☐ c. paint.

2. Molly is very
   - ☐ a. tall.
   - ☐ b. messy.
   - ☐ c. neat.

3. When Molly drew the line, she was
   - ☐ a. angry.
   - ☐ b. playful.
   - ☐ c. selfish.

4. Molly thought her sister was
   - ☐ a. a slob.
   - ☐ b. too neat.
   - ☐ c. her best friend.

5. When the sisters lived in town, they
   - ☐ a. were better friends.
   - ☐ b. shared a room.
   - ☐ c. had separate bedrooms.

6. Dad thought it was unacademic to
   - ☐ a. generalize.
   - ☐ b. dream.
   - ☐ c. complain.

7. When Molly is grown up, she wants to be a
   - ☐ a. person who has done something important.
   - ☐ b. teacher.
   - ☐ c. wife and mother.

114

8. How does the narrator feel?
   □ a. self-confident
   □ b. determined and unsure
   □ c. downright smug

✏ _____ Number of correct answers
Enter this number on the Comprehension graph on page 132.

Critical Thinking

Put an ✗ in the box next to the best answer for each question or statement. You may look back at the selection if you'd like.

1. The author intended this story to be
   □ a. funny.
   □ b. serious.
   □ c. sad.

2. Who is the narrator of this story?
   □ a. Meg
   □ b. Molly
   □ c. Dad

3. For the narrator, the hardest part about sharing a room is that she has
   □ a. no space for her belongings.
   □ b. no privacy.
   □ c. trouble sleeping.

4. As they grow older, you can predict that Meg and Molly will
   □ a. no longer be friends.
   □ b. become more alike.
   □ c. become more different.

5. The line was drawn across the room so that
   □ a. Molly could be messy in her space.
   □ b. Meg would have a clean space.
   □ c. Molly would have a clean space.

6. Which of the following is a statement of opinion rather than fact?
   □ a. When we lived in town, we both had our own rooms.
   □ b. The hardest part about living in the same room with someone is that it's hard to keep anything hidden.
   □ c. It was Molly who drew the line.

7. Meg and Molly are
   □ a. very different.
   □ b. very much alike.
   □ c. alike in some ways.

8. The narrator spends a lot of time
   □ a. painting.
   □ b. cleaning.
   □ c. thinking.

✏ _____ Number of correct answers
Enter this number on the Critical Thinking graph on page 133.

Vocabulary

Each numbered sentence contains an underlined word from the selection. Following are three definitions. Put an ✗ in the box next to the best meaning of the word as it is used in the sentence.

1. It didn't really make us better friends, but it gave us the chance to <u>ignore</u> each other more.
   □ a. love
   □ b. forget
   □ c. see

2. She's <u>content</u>, waiting for that; I'm restless, and so impatient.
   □ a. happy
   □ b. full
   □ c. impatient

3. She's sure, <u>absolutely</u> sure, that what she's waiting for will happen, just the way she wants it to.
   - ☐ a. never
   - ☐ b. completely
   - ☐ c. sometimes

4. Molly is calm, easygoing, self-confident, downright <u>smug</u>.
   - ☐ a. self-satisfied
   - ☐ b. weak
   - ☐ c. tearful

5. Being both determined and unsure at the same time is what makes me the way I am, I think: hasty, <u>impetuous</u>, sometimes angry over nothing.
   - ☐ a. cruel
   - ☐ b. careful
   - ☐ c. thoughtless

6. Being so well sorted out in her goals, and so <u>assured</u> of everything happening the way she wants and expects it to, is what makes Molly the way she is.
   - ☐ a. convinced
   - ☐ b. afraid
   - ☐ c. tired

7. I mean the parts of yourself that are private: the tears you want to <u>shed</u> sometimes for no reason.
   - ☐ a. hide
   - ☐ b. spill
   - ☐ c. stop

8. You want to think in a <u>solitary</u> place, say words you want to say aloud to hear how they sound, but only to yourself.
   - ☐ a. crowded
   - ☐ b. lonely
   - ☐ c. foreign

✎ _____ **Number of correct answers**
Enter this number on the Vocabulary graph on page 134.

Personal Response

I can understand how Meg feels because

_____

_____

_____

One way I am like (Meg/Molly) is

_____

_____

_____

28 | The Martial Arts

by Susan Ribner and Dr. Richard Chin

In this passage, the authors relate a very old tale as a way to introduce you to the ancient origins of the martial arts.

Centuries ago in China a small old man with a long beard was walking through the woods, leaning on a gnarled walking stick. At a turn in the path he found three bandits attacking a poor peasant who was on his way home from market. The old man approached the bandits slowly and said in a soft but firm voice, "Stop. Leave that man alone."

"Go away, old man. Mind your own business!" commanded the leader of the bandits, a towering, bearlike man.

Calmly the old man replied, "Don't you know that if you do evil, evil will come back to you?"

"Stop preaching, old man, or I'll smash you like this," said the huge man, and kicked at a nearby tree, smashing it in half.

The old man smiled faintly. "I do not fear you," he said.

With that, this headstrong bandit lost his temper and kicked out at the small man. Seemingly without effort, the old man brushed aside the kick, and the bandit went crashing on his back in the dust.

The second bandit, a tall, wiry woman with piercing eyes, drew her sword and rushed toward the old man. She slashed at the man's head, but before she completed the move, the old man had already moved out of range. The woman turned around to see the third bandit, who had tried to tackle the old man's legs, go flying through the air and land in a big puddle of mud.

The three bandits, now outraged at this humiliation, growled, cursed, made fierce faces, and attacked the old man all at once.

But the little man could not be touched, and the three bandits landed in a heap.

Realizing that they were in the presence of a master, the three fell to their knees and begged the old man to forgive them. "Take us as your students, please, teach us what you know."

"I cannot teach you my fighting art," said the old man, "for this art cannot be given to those who will use it to bully other people. The martial arts are for those of good character who will protect people from bullies like you. In fact, if you do not have the right attitude, I could teach you for the rest of my life and yours, and you still would not comprehend this art."

The three bandits continued to plead, and promised they would change their ways and give up their bandit lives. After they apologized to the much-relieved peasant, the bandits and the old man walked off into the woods together.

We do not know what became of the three bandits, but we do know that what happened in this story is symbolically important in the history of the martial arts. For this old man was a kung fu master of the Shaolin monastery. Around the year A.D. 600, he and other monks and nuns of that order—some of the great kung fu masters of their time—developed the fighting arts in ways never attempted before, and in a manner that profoundly influenced the martial arts as we know them today.

According to legend, about 1,500 years ago, a Buddhist monk traveled several thousand miles from India into China, walking alone over the Himalaya Mountains, through forests filled with wild animals, through swamps, over unbridged rivers. His name was Bodhidarma, and he was to found what is now known as Zen Buddhism.

After receiving permission from the Chinese emperor to remain in China, Bodhidarma traveled to a Buddhist monastery in Honan Province. This monastery, hidden away in the middle of a green forest, was called Shaolin. Bodhidarma began to instruct the monks in his way of Buddhism, but he found that they were so weak from their inactive life in the monastery that they would fall asleep during the meditations he was trying to teach them. So Bodhidarma proceeded to give the monks certain exercises to make them healthier and stronger, telling them they could never become spiritually strong if they were physically weak.

These new exercises—special hand movements, body positions, and breathing exercises—also turned out to be useful as self-defense techniques. One of the exercises the monks practiced was standing in a special position called Horse-Riding Stance. It was called this because the position resembled how one looks sitting on a horse—both legs wide apart, knees bent, and back straight. The Shaolin monks practiced this exercise by standing in Horse-Riding Stance for as long as one hour at a time. ■

✔ Enter your reading time below. Then look up your reading speed on the Words-per-Minute table on page 130.

Reading Time _____

Reading Speed _____

Enter your reading speed on the Reading Speed graph on page 131.

Comprehension

Put an **X** in the box next to the correct answer for each question or statement. Do not look back at the selection.

1. The story of the old man and the bandits took place in
   - ☐ a. India.
   - ☐ b. China.
   - ☐ c. Japan.

2. The old man told the bandits that he could not teach them his fighting art because
   - ☐ a. they could not pay him.
   - ☐ b. he had too many students.
   - ☐ c. they would use it to bully others.

3. Who was the old man?
   - ☐ a. a poor peasant
   - ☐ b. a kung fu master
   - ☐ c. an emperor

4. The bandits
   - ☐ a. robbed the old man.
   - ☐ b. begged the old man to forgive them.
   - ☐ c. ran away.

5. Shaolin was a
   - ☐ a. Buddhist monk.
   - ☐ b. kind of martial art.
   - ☐ c. monastery.

6. The authors believed that the most important development of the fighting arts occurred around the year A.D.
   - ☐ a. 600.
   - ☐ b. 1500.
   - ☐ c. 1850.

7. Bodhidarma founded
   - ☐ a. kung fu.
   - ☐ b. Zen Buddhism.
   - ☐ c. Shaolin.

8. Bodhidarma wanted the monks and nuns to be physically strong so they could
   - ☐ a. be spiritually strong.
   - ☐ b. defend themselves.
   - ☐ c. work in the fields.

✎ _____ Number of correct answers
Enter this number on the Comprehension graph on page 132.

Critical Thinking

Put an **X** in the box next to the best answer for each question or statement. You may look back at the selection if you'd like.

1. The author's main purpose in writing this selection was to
   - ☐ a. inform you of some of the history of the martial art of kung fu.
   - ☐ b. instruct you in some of the techniques of kung fu.
   - ☐ c. persuade you that kung fu is an art you should learn.

2. Which is the most important idea in the selection?
   - ☐ a. Martial arts can be useful for self-defense.
   - ☐ b. Kung fu can help you win fights.
   - ☐ c. It is important to be physically strong as well as spiritually strong.

3. The story of the old man took place
   - ☐ a. more than 100 years ago.
   - ☐ b. more than 1,000 years ago.
   - ☐ c. less than 100 years ago.

4. Which event happened first?
   - ☐ a. The old man fought three bandits in the woods.
   - ☐ b. Bodhidarma traveled to Shaolin and began to instruct the monks in his way of Buddhism.
   - ☐ c. The old man and other monks and nuns developed the fighting arts in ways never attempted before.

5. The bandits attacked the old man because he
   - ☐ a. was protecting the peasant.
   - ☐ b. had insulted them.
   - ☐ c. was very rich.

6. Although the bandits outnumbered the old man, he
   - ☐ a. had friends to help him.
   - ☐ b. was much bigger.
   - ☐ c. used kung fu to defeat them.

7. Which of the following does *not* fit with the other two?
   - ☐ a. Shaolin
   - ☐ b. kung fu
   - ☐ c. Zen Buddhism

8. Shaolin monks practiced the Horse-Riding Stance for as long as an hour at a time in order to
   - ☐ a. improve their posture.
   - ☐ b. improve their horseback riding.
   - ☐ c. become stronger.

✎ _____ Number of correct answers
Enter this number on the Critical Thinking graph on page 133.

Vocabulary

Each numbered sentence contains an underlined word from the selection. Following are three definitions. Put an **✗** in the box next to the best meaning of the word as it is used in the sentence.

1. Centuries ago in China a small old man with a long beard was walking through the woods, leaning on a <u>gnarled</u> walking stick.
   - ☐ a. twisted
   - ☐ b. broken
   - ☐ c. metal

2. With that, this <u>headstrong</u> bandit lost his temper and kicked out at the small man.
   - ☐ a. simple
   - ☐ b. clever
   - ☐ c. impatient

3. <u>Seemingly</u> without effort, the old man brushed aside the kick, and the bandit went crashing on his back in the dust.
   - ☐ a. easily
   - ☐ b. apparently
   - ☐ c. painfully

4. The three bandits, now <u>outraged</u> at this humiliation, growled, cursed, made fierce faces, and attacked the old man.
   - ☐ a. calm
   - ☐ b. upset
   - ☐ c. concerned

5. The three bandits continued to <u>plead</u>, and promised to change their ways.
   - ☐ a. cough
   - ☐ b. fight
   - ☐ c. beg

6. "In fact, if you do not have the right attitude, I could teach you for the rest of my life and yours, and you still would not <u>comprehend</u> this art."
   - ☐ a. understand
   - ☐ b. purchase
   - ☐ c. steal

7. The great kung fu master developed the fighting arts in a manner that <u>profoundly</u> influenced the martial arts.
   - ☐ a. never
   - ☐ b. barely
   - ☐ c. deeply

8. It was called this because the position <u>resembles</u> how one looks sitting on a horse—both legs wide apart, knees bent, and back straight.
   - ☐ a. appears like
   - ☐ b. sounds like
   - ☐ c. stands on

✎ _____ **Number of correct answers**
Enter this number on the Vocabulary graph on page 134.

Personal Response

Would you like to learn one of the various forms of the martial arts? Why or why not?

_____

_____

If you could ask the authors one question about the martial arts, what would it be?

_____

_____

29 | Island of the Blue Dolphins

by Scott O'Dell

Island of the Blue Dolphins tells about the life of Karana, a Native American girl, who was accidentally left behind after her people migrated from one island to another. In this passage the lonely Karana, having given up all hope of being rescued, decides to try to escape from the island.

Summer is the best time on the Island of the Blue Dolphins. The sun is warm then and the winds blow milder out of the west, sometimes out of the south.

It was during these days that the ship might return and now I spent most of my time on the rock, looking out from the high headland into the east, toward the country where my people had gone, across the sea that was never-ending.

Once while I watched I saw a small object which I took to be the ship, but a stream of water rose from it and I knew that it was a whale spouting. During those summer days I saw nothing else.

The first storm of winter ended my hopes. If the white men's ship were coming for me it would have come during the time of good weather. Now I would have to wait until winter was gone, maybe longer.

The thought of being alone on the island while so many suns rose from the sea and went slowly back into the sea filled my heart with loneliness. I had not felt so lonely before because I was sure that the ship would return as Matasaip had said it would. Now my hopes were dead. Now I was really alone. I could not eat much, nor could I sleep without dreaming terrible dreams.

The storm blew out of the north, sending big waves against the island and winds so strong that I was unable to stay on the rock. I moved my bed to the foot of the rock and for protection kept a fire going throughout the night. I slept there five times. The first night the dogs came and stood outside the ring made by the fire. I killed three of them with arrows, but not the leader, and they did not come again.

On the sixth day, when the storm had ended, I went to the place where the canoes had been hidden, and let myself down over the cliff. This part of the shore was sheltered from the wind and I found the canoes just as they had been left. The dried food was still good, but the water was stale, so I went back to the spring and filled a fresh basket.

I had decided during the days of the storm, when I had given up hope of seeing the ship, that I would take one of the canoes and go to the country that lay toward the east. I remembered how Kimki, before he had gone, had asked the advice of his ancestors who had lived many ages in the past, who had come to the island from that country, and likewise the advice of Zuma, the medicine man who held power over the wind and the seas. But these things I could not do, for Zuma had been killed by the Aleuts, and in all my life I had never been able to speak with the dead.

I cannot say that I was really afraid as I stood there on the shore. I knew that my ancestors had crossed the sea in their canoes, coming from that place which lay beyond. Kimki, too, had crossed the sea. I was not nearly so skilled with a canoe as these men, but I must say that whatever might befall me on the endless waters did not trouble me. It meant far less than the thought of staying on the island alone, without a home or companions, pursued by wild dogs, where everything reminded me of those who were dead and those who had gone away.

Of the four canoes stored there against the cliff, I chose the smallest, which was still very heavy because it could carry six people. The task that faced me was to push it down the rocky shore and into the water, a distance four or five times its length.

This I did by first removing all the large rocks in front of the canoe. I then filled in all these holes with pebbles and along this path laid down long strips of kelp, making a slippery bed. The shore was steep and once I got the canoe to move with its own weight, it slid down the path and into the water.

The sun was in the west when I left the shore. The sea was calm behind the high cliffs. Using the two-bladed paddle I quickly skirted the south part of the island. ■

✔ Enter your reading time below. Then look up your reading speed on the Words-per-Minute table on page 130.

Reading Time _____

Reading Speed _____

Enter your reading speed on the Reading Speed graph on page 131.

Comprehension

Put an **X** in the box next to the correct answer for each question or statement. Do not look back at the selection.

1. During the summer, the winds on the island blow
   - ☐ a. milder.
   - ☐ b. harder.
   - ☐ c. out of the north.

2. While Karana watched the ocean, she saw
   - ☐ a. a ship.
   - ☐ b. a whale.
   - ☐ c. schools of dolphins.

3. Before winter came, Karana had not felt so lonely because
   - ☐ a. the dogs were company for her.
   - ☐ b. she had enjoyed being alone.
   - ☐ c. she was sure that the ship would return to get her.

4. For protection against the wild dogs, Karana
   - ☐ a. made a fence around the camp.
   - ☐ b. made a circle of rocks around her camp.
   - ☐ c. kept a fire going all night.

5. When the dogs approached Karana's camp, she
   - ☐ a. killed three of them with arrows.
   - ☐ b. killed only the leader.
   - ☐ c. threw stones at them to chase them away.

6. Who was Zuma?
   - ☐ a. the chief of the tribe
   - ☐ b. the medicine man
   - ☐ c. a close friend of Karana

7. The thought of what could happen to her on the open sea did not trouble Karana as much as the thought of being
   - ☐ a. alone on the island without home or companions.
   - ☐ b. without food or water.
   - ☐ c. killed by wild dogs.

8. Karana decided to row a canoe to the east to
   - ☐ a. find her people.
   - ☐ b. find fresh water.
   - ☐ c. trade for food.

✎ _____ Number of correct answers
Enter this number on the Comprehension graph on page 132.

Critical Thinking

Put an ✗ in the box next to the best answer for each question or statement. You may look back at the selection if you'd like.

1. The author intended this selection to be
   - ☐ a. a humorous story.
   - ☐ b. a mystery story.
   - ☐ c. an adventure story.

2. Who is the narrator of this story?
   - ☐ a. Zuma, the medicine man
   - ☐ b. Karana, the Native American girl
   - ☐ c. an outside observer

3. More than anything else, Karana hoped to see
   - ☐ a. her mother.
   - ☐ b. a ship.
   - ☐ c. her tribe.

4. Which word best describes Karana?
   - ☐ a. afraid
   - ☐ b. determined
   - ☐ c. angry

5. Karana's terrible dreams were caused by
   - ☐ a. her loneliness.
   - ☐ b. her fear.
   - ☐ c. the wild dogs.

6. Which event happened first?
   - ☐ a. Karana killed some wild dogs.
   - ☐ b. Karana thought she saw a ship.
   - ☐ c. Karana went to the place where the canoes were hidden.

7. What caused Karana to attempt to cross the sea in a canoe?
   - ☐ a. She feared the wild dogs would kill her.
   - ☐ b. She was running out of food.
   - ☐ c. She had given up hope of being rescued by a ship.

8. Karana really wasn't afraid at the thought of crossing the sea in a canoe because she
   - ☐ a. knew her ancestors had crossed the sea in canoes before.
   - ☐ b. was an expert in handling a canoe.
   - ☐ c. knew she didn't have to travel very far.

✎ _____ Number of correct answers
Enter this number on the Critical Thinking graph on page 133.

Vocabulary

Each numbered sentence contains an underlined word from the selection. Following are three definitions. Put an ✗ in the box next to the best meaning of the word as it is used in the sentence.

1. The sun is warm then and the winds blow <u>milder</u> out of the west.
   - ☐ a. gentler
   - ☐ b. stormier
   - ☐ c. cooler

2. I saw a small object which I took to be the ship, but a stream of water rose from it and I knew that it was a whale <u>spouting</u>.
   - ☐ a. swimming
   - ☐ b. calling
   - ☐ c. spraying

3. I remembered how Kimki, before he had gone, had asked the advice of his ancestors who had lived many <u>ages</u> in the past.
   - ☐ a. months
   - ☐ b. years
   - ☐ c. times

4. I was not nearly so <u>skilled</u> with a canoe as these men.
   - ☐ a. quick
   - ☐ b. clumsy
   - ☐ c. well-trained

5. I must say that whatever might <u>befall</u> me on the endless waters did not trouble me.
   - ☐ a. come to
   - ☐ b. pass by
   - ☐ c. happen to

6. It meant far less than the thought of staying on the island alone, without a home or companions, <u>pursued</u> by wild dogs.
   - ☐ a. befriended
   - ☐ b. called
   - ☐ c. chased

7. The <u>task</u> that faced me was to push it down the rocky shore and into the water.
   - ☐ a. job
   - ☐ b. threat
   - ☐ c. fun

8. Using the two-bladed paddle I quickly <u>skirted</u> the south part of the island.
   - ☐ a. sped toward
   - ☐ b. went around
   - ☐ c. traveled across

✎ _____ Number of correct answers
Enter this number on the Vocabulary graph on page 134.

Personal Response

What do you think of Karana's plan to leave the island? Explain.

_____

_____

_____

What three things would you miss the most if you were marooned on a desert island?

_____

_____

_____

30 | The Native American Meets the Horse

by GaWaNi Pony Boy

For centuries humans and animals have worked together. But no relationship has been stronger than the bond that developed between Native Americans and their horses.

Native Americans respect and admire every bird, fish, rock, and plant just as you respect and admire close family members. If you have ever had a long-term relationship with an animal, you probably know the love that grows with this relationship. Horses have been viewed by Native Americans as companions and animals to be cared for. And sometimes the horse was also a messenger, teacher, or guide.

Native Americans lived for thousands of years without horses. Let's go back in time and find out how Native Americans first met the horse.

Ancestors of the horse lived in North America 40 million years ago. But 15,000 years ago during the Ice Age, the last of these prehistoric animals crossed a land bridge from what is now Alaska to Siberia. There, on the other side of the Pacific Ocean, they roamed over the grasslands of Asia and were domesticated.

Eventually, these domesticated horses were traded westward across Europe and North Africa. When the Spaniards came to explore the New World, they loaded horses onto boats and brought them to North America. Explorers Christopher Columbus, Ponce de León, and Hernando de Soto all brought horses with them.

Before horses were brought back to North America, Native Americans used dogs in everyday life. Dogs are loyal, good hunters, and they helped transport family belongings. Although Native Americans were never true nomads, some tribes moved from summer camps to winter camps. When moving, two large sticks were crossed and tied to a dog's back, forming a travois on which family belongings could be tied.

Using dogs for moving wasn't easy. Can you imagine packing all your family's belongings and loading them onto a travois tied to your dog's back instead of getting a moving van? A dog can pack 30 to 40 pounds at best, and walk only 5 to 6 miles per day. And a dog needs to eat meat. Besides that, dogs often fight with each other, and if a rabbit should run across the path, a dog—along with all of its cargo—would take off after it.

When Native Americans first saw horses, they described them as being giant dogs. Gradually, several Indian tribes began to understand the strange animals by watching how the Spaniards used them. But when Native Americans in New Mexico drove out the Spanish settlers and captured their sheep, cattle, and horses, they questioned the horse's value. After all, horses ate what little grass there was available for sheep. And it was the sheep, not horses, who could provide meat and wool. So the Southwestern tribes traded the horses to tribes in the north and east.

Many horses escaped captivity and migrated to an area that is now Idaho, Oregon, and Washington. Horses lived well in this region. Snow-capped mountains served as a natural fence line, guarding horses against such enemies as wolves and puma. All around were fields of green grass and mountain streams, so the horses had plenty to eat and drink.

Native peoples in these areas immediately saw how to use the horse to make life easier. A horse can carry 200 pounds on its back or drag 300 pounds on a travois. A horse can travel more than 20 miles a day and needs only grass to eat. And horses are relatively peaceful among themselves. Once tamed, horses are more dependable, easier to handle, and require less care than do dogs.

With the introduction of the horse, Native American life changed dramatically. On horseback, buffalo could be chased and hunted with great speed, increasing a hunter's chance of success. Hunting territories expanded with the increased ability to track, chase, and successfully hunt buffalo. Riderless horses were used as runners. Runners were trained to run, or chase, a herd of buffalo in the direction of the hunters while the hunters waited atop fresh mounts.

The Shoshoni tribe in Idaho was one of the first to see the value of having horses, but the Nez Percé quickly caught on. An unlikely people to even want horses because the Nez Percé mainly fished for salmon in the beautiful, clear north rivers, they simply liked the horse—especially the spotted ones. So some villages combined their resources and bought several from the Shoshoni.

The Nez Percé didn't waste any time. They began breeding their top mares with their top stallions. They wanted horses that were not only swift and surefooted but also calm and even-tempered. This was important for hunting and fighting in wars. ■

✔ **Enter your reading time below. Then look up your reading speed on the Words-per-Minute table on page 130.**

Reading Time _____

Reading Speed _____

Enter your reading speed on the Reading Speed graph on page 131.

Comprehension

Put an **X** in the box next to the correct answer for each question or statement. Do not look back at the selection.

1. During the Ice Age, prehistoric horses left North America and crossed into
   □ a. Europe.
   □ b. Siberia.
   □ c. Alaska.

2. Horses were brought back to North America by
   □ a. ancestors of Native Americans.
   □ b. Alaskan Eskimos.
   □ c. Spanish explorers.

3. What animals did Native Americans use for everyday work before they had horses?
   □ a. dogs
   □ b. buffalo
   □ c. mules

4. The Southwestern tribes believed that horses were not as valuable as were
   □ a. sheep.
   □ b. cattle.
   □ c. dogs.

5. How far can horses travel in a single day?
   □ a. five to six miles
   □ b. about 15 miles
   □ c. more than 20 miles

6. Horses increased the Native Americans' chances for success when they chased and hunted
   - ☐ a. wolves.
   - ☐ b. buffalo.
   - ☐ c. sheep.

7. One of the first tribes to see the value of having horses was the
   - ☐ a. Shoshoni.
   - ☐ b. Southwestern groups.
   - ☐ c. Nez Percé.

8. Why did it seem unlikely that the Nez Percé would even want horses?
   - ☐ a. They mainly fished for salmon.
   - ☐ b. They mainly raised sheep.
   - ☐ c. They preferred to use dogs to help with their everyday work.

✎ _____ Number of correct answers
Enter this number on the Comprehension graph on page 132.

Critical Thinking

Put an **X** in the box next to the best answer for each question or statement. You may look back at the selection if you'd like.

1. What was the author's purpose in writing this selection?
   - ☐ a. to explain the history of the horse in North America
   - ☐ b. to emphasize how much more Native Americans valued horses than dogs
   - ☐ c. to inform you how Native Americans first met horses and how the relationship grew

2. Compared to dogs, horses
   - ☐ a. are harder to handle
   - ☐ b. are more dependable
   - ☐ c. require more care

3. Using dogs for moving wasn't easy because they
   - ☐ a. were too lazy.
   - ☐ b. often fought with each other.
   - ☐ c. only wanted to hunt.

4. Which event happened first?
   - ☐ a. Southwestern tribes traded horses to other tribes.
   - ☐ b. The Spaniards brought horses to the New World.
   - ☐ c. Horses roamed the grasslands of Asia.

5. Southwestern tribes traded their horses to other tribes because the horses
   - ☐ a. ate grass that their sheep needed.
   - ☐ b. took too long to tame.
   - ☐ c. were difficult to ride.

6. Compared to dogs, horses require
   - ☐ a. no care.
   - ☐ b. less care.
   - ☐ c. more care.

7. Which of the following does *not* fit with the other two?
   - ☐ a. Nez Percé
   - ☐ b. Shoshoni
   - ☐ c. Spaniards

8. Which word best describes Native Americans' feeling about horses?
   - ☐ a. annoyance
   - ☐ b. fear
   - ☐ c. reverence

✎ _____ Number of correct answers
Enter this number on the Critical Thinking graph on page 133.

Vocabulary

Each numbered sentence contains an underlined word from the selection. Following are three definitions. Put an **✗** in the box next to the best meaning of the word as it is used in the sentence.

1. They roamed over the grasslands of Asia and were <u>domesticated</u>.
   - ☐ a. captured
   - ☐ b. tamed
   - ☐ c. made wild

2. <u>Eventually</u>, these domesticated horses were traded westward.
   - ☐ a. finally
   - ☐ b. unfortunately
   - ☐ c. normally

3. Although Native Americans were never true <u>nomads</u>, some tribes moved from summer camps to winter camps.
   - ☐ a. hunters
   - ☐ b. horseman
   - ☐ c. wanderers

4. The Southwestern tribes <u>traded</u> the horses to groups in the north and east.
   - ☐ a. exchanged
   - ☐ b. gave away
   - ☐ c. sold

5. Many horses escaped captivity and <u>migrated</u> to an area that is now Idaho, Oregon, and Washington.
   - ☐ a. returned
   - ☐ b. traded
   - ☐ c. moved

6. Once tamed, horses are more <u>dependable</u>, easier to handle, and require less care than do dogs.
   - ☐ a. excitable
   - ☐ b. reliable
   - ☐ c. stubborn

7. Hunting territories <u>expanded</u> with the increased ability to track, chase, and successfully hunt buffalo.
   - ☐ a. became larger
   - ☐ b. became smaller
   - ☐ c. were moved

8. So some villages <u>combined</u> their resources and bought several from the Shosoni.
   - ☐ a. separated
   - ☐ b. joined together
   - ☐ c. harvested

✎ _____ **Number of correct answers**
Enter this number on the Vocabulary graph on page 134.

Personal Response

Describe a close relationship that you have had with an animal.

_____

_____

_____

✔ **Check Your Progress**
Study the graphs you completed for Lessons 21–30 and answer the How Am I Doing? questions on page 137.

Assessment

Words per Minute

Reading Time	Words per Minute	Reading Time	Words per Minute
1:00	750	4:40	161
1:10	647	4:50	155
1:20	564	**5:00**	150
1:30	500	5:10	145
1:40	452	5:20	141
1:50	410	5:30	136
2:00	375	5:40	133
2:10	347	5:50	129
2:20	322	**6:00**	125
2:30	300	6:10	122
2:40	282	6:20	118
2:50	265	6:30	115
3:00	250	6:40	113
3:10	237	6:50	110
3:20	225	**7:00**	107
3:30	214	7:10	105
3:40	205	7:20	102
3:50	196	7:30	100
4:00	188	7:40	98
4:10	180	7:50	96
4:20	173	**8:00**	94
4:30	167		

Reading Speed

Directions. Use the graph below to show your reading speed improvement.

First, along the top of the graph, find the lesson number of the selection you just read. Then put a small X on the line directly below the number of the lesson and across from the number of words per minute you read.

As you mark your speed for each lesson, graph your progress by drawing a line to connect the X's. This will help you see right away whether your reading speed is going up as it should be. If the line connecting the X's is not going up, see your teacher for advice.

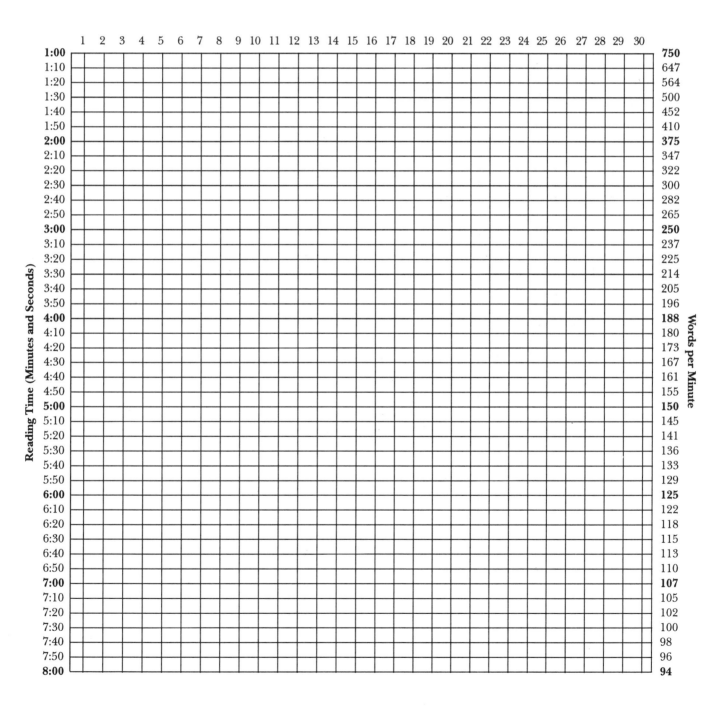

Comprehension

Directions. Use the graph below to show your comprehension scores.

First, along the top of the graph, find the lesson number of the selection you just read. Then put a small **X** on the line directly below the number of the lesson and across from the score you earned.

As you mark your score for each lesson, graph your progress by drawing a line to connect the X's. This will help you see right away whether your comprehension scores are going up or down. If your scores are below 75%, or if they are going down, see your teacher. Try to keep your scores at 75% or above while you continue to build your reading speed.

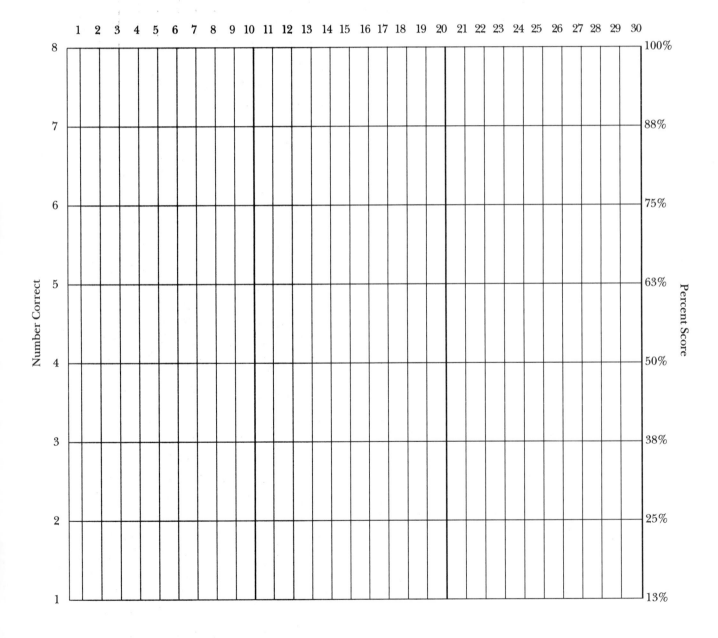

Critical Thinking

Directions. Use the graph below to show your critical thinking scores.

First, along the top of the graph, find the lesson number of the selection you just read. Then put a small X on the line directly below the number of the lesson and across from the score you earned.

As you mark your score for each lesson, graph your progress by drawing a line to connect the X's. This will help you see right away whether your critical thinking scores are going up or down. If your scores are below 75%, or if they are going down, see your teacher. Try to keep your scores at 75% or above as you continue to build your reading speed.

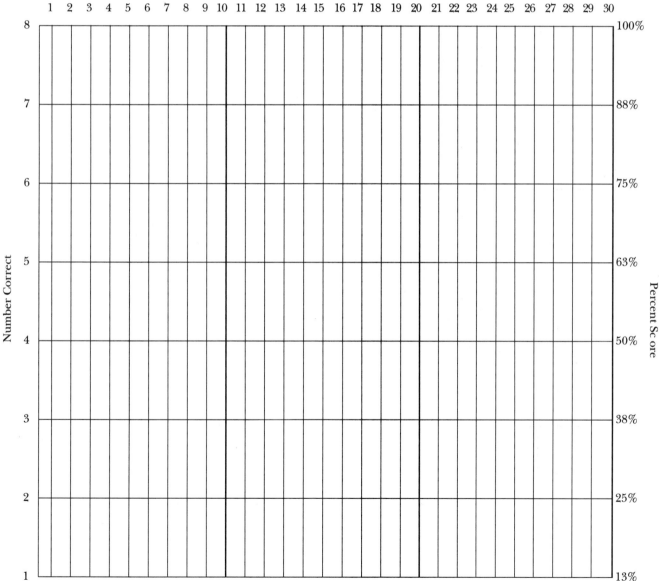

Vocabulary

Directions. Use the graph below to show your vocabulary scores.

First, along the top of the graph, find the lesson number of the selection you just read. Then put a small X on the line directly below the number of the lesson and across from the score you earned.

As you mark your score for each lesson, graph your progress by drawing a line to connect the X's. This will help you see right away whether your vocabulary scores are going up or down. If your scores are not going up, see your teacher for advice. Vocabulary scores of 75% are good, but try to earn scores of 88% and 100% when you can.

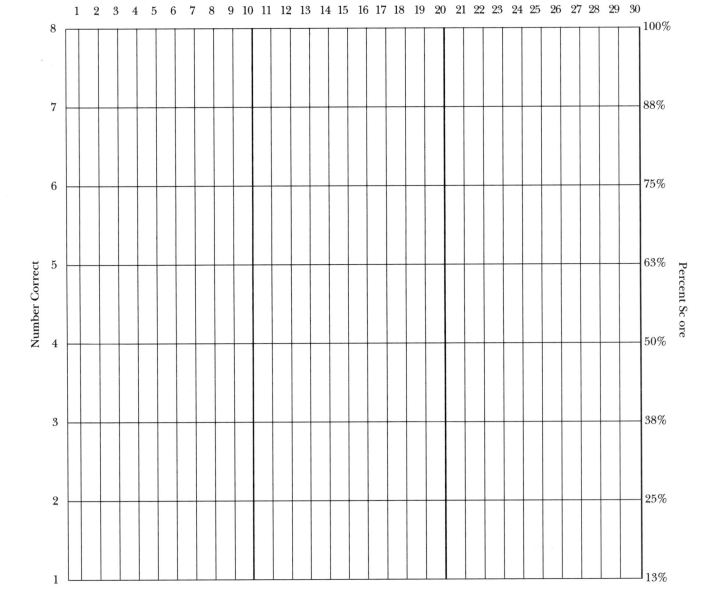

How Am I Doing?

Lessons 1—10

1. Which lesson are you most proud of? Why?

   _____

   _____

   _____

2. Which lesson did you find most difficult? Why was it difficult?

   _____

   _____

   _____

3. Which type of exercises did you do best: Comprehension, Critical Thinking, or Vocabulary? Why do you think this is true?

   _____

   _____

   _____

4. What skills or strategies will you use to improve your scores in the following lessons?

   _____

   _____

   _____

5. How can you continue to improve your reading speed and comprehension in the following lessons?

   _____

   _____

   _____

How Am I Doing?

Lessons 11–20

1. How does your reading speed for nonfiction selections compare with your reading speed for fiction? Explain.

   _____

   _____

   _____

2. When you read faster do your comprehension scores go up or down? What do you think may be happening?

   _____

   _____

   _____

3. What lesson was most confusing for you? Why?

   _____

   _____

   _____

4. What do you like or dislike about the personal response questions? Explain.

   _____

   _____

   _____

5. What have you improved upon the most in Lessons 11–20?

   _____

   _____

   _____

How Am I Doing?

Lessons 21—30

1. Did your reading speed increase as you completed the lessons in this book? Explain why you think it did or did not.

_____

_____

_____

_____

2. How has your everyday reading changed since you began these lessons? Explain and be specific.

_____

_____

_____

_____

3. Overall, what was most difficult about the lessons in this book? What was easiest? Explain both answers.

_____

_____

_____

_____

4. How has completing these lessons affected your everyday reading? Do you read more books for pleasure? Have you been able to read faster and understand concepts better in your textbooks? Are you enjoying reading more? Explain and be specific.

_____

_____

_____

_____